BRITISH
WARSHIPS
& AUXILIARIES

HMS Bulwark leads MV Hurst Point through the Suez Canal

THE ROYAL NAVY

Each year I take this opportunity to conduct a brief health check of the Royal Navy - how it is coping today and what issues it is likely to face in the future. It is well documented that in the recent past the RN has endured a series of brutal cuts to both capability and number of major warships - yet demand for these ships for worldwide operations remains undiminished. A quick snapshot, taken as I write this in November 2013, shows 16 warships deployed, supported by eight RFAs. Of that number of warships and RFAs 16 were deployed east of Suez - some conducting anti-piracy operations off the Horn of Africa; others exercises and operations in the gulf region and DARING in the Far East. A further nine warships were deployed on operations or training in and around the UK. The recent cuts have left the RN severely short of warships - particularly the workhorses of the fleet, the destroyers and frigates; those ships able to deploy for extended periods to distant stations and able to conduct the widest range of warfare roles. Not so long ago, the minimum number of such vessels considered necessary to perform their worldwide commitments was stated to be 32. Today that number has declined to just 19 - comprising the six Type 45 destroyers and the remaining 13 Type 23 frigates - and not all of these can be operational at any one time. With the Type 45 build programme completed and the Type 26 frigate programme getting underway it is unlikely that the escort fleet will see an increase in numbers any time soon. It has been said that the Type 26s will replace the Type 23s on a one-for-one basis - that would be good, but remember that the government promised that the 12 Type 42 destroyers would be similarly replaced by the Type 45 but in the event, terminology was soon changed to "twelve ships", then "up to twelve ships", followed by "eight ships" and eventually delivering just six, though to the government's mind, increased capability meant that each new ship was as good as two old ships, yet still missing the vital point that a single ship cannot be in two places at once.

2014 is the last year of the first five-year phase of the Strategic Defence and Security Review, a Defence Review intended to lay the footprint for the Future Force 2020. A second review is due to take place in 2015. It is widely considered that SDSR was flawed in both message and implementation. It was sold to the military, and the public, as a bottom up restructuring of the Armed Forces, based on a future strategy of smaller, more mobile forces, able to rapidly deploy and respond to world events, wherever they may occur - however within months the Arab spring was in full flow, catching the government on the hop and having to extend the service of some ships and aircraft which were on their way into retirement. As the government began dismantling whole capabilites before replacements were in place, commentators soon realised that the proposed streamlining of forces was nothing more than window dressing designed to conceal yet more savage defence cuts. UK Defence Strategy was playing second fiddle to the need to cut expenditure. The carrier strike capability was removed from the order of battle. The fixed wing strike capability offered by the Harrier was abruptly terminated by the withdrawal of the aircraft from active service and the decommissioning of ARK ROYAL; Airborne Maritime Patrol was consigned to history as the Nimrod MRA4 programme was cancelled and the aircraft arbitrarily destroyed; the Sea King aircraft is to leave service in 2016 which will leave the RN without airborne early warning until a decision is made about a replacement system - probably fitted to a Merlin airframe, but not expected to enter service any time before 2022!

So where are the RN now? There are several major capital programmes underway which will deliver much needed capability, but these are not without issues. The Queen Elizabeth class aircraft carriers are well underway, with the first ship QUEEN ELIZABETH now structurally complete and scheduled to be floated up in 2014. The empty dry dock at Rosyth will then allow the various mega blocks of the second carrier PRINCE OF WALES, already under construction, to be moved to Rosyth for assembly. Despite headlines in the National Press of spiralling costs and protracted delays, the design and building of these two vessels, the largest warships ever built for the RN, has in reality been relatively trouble free - the Aircraft Carrier Alliance has pulled off a wonderful feat of co-ordination and construction in bringing together the blocks built at shipyards around the UK and scheduling a complex build at Rosyth. It is true that the build has over-run and it is also true that the original budget has been exceeded, possibly even doubled, but little of this can be laid at the door of the contractors. The government requested a revised delivery schedule, slowing the build of the ships so that their in-service date coincided with the availability of the F-35 aircraft that is to operate from their decks; the government requested that the design be changed to incorporate catapults and arrestor wires to accommodate the F-35C variant of the lightning, before changing their minds and reverting to the F-35B. All of this causes additional expense and delay - it is unfair to paint the contractor as the villain as they could have delivered a fantastic ship on schedule had the government not have kept moving the goalposts. So the wait for a new carrier strike capability is not that far away - QUEEN ELIZABETH, now structurally complete will, by the end of the year, be afloat and fitting out. However, the speed of advance with the carrier construction has not been mirrored by a similar speed with the F-35 procurement.

As we went to press in November, the government had yet to order F-35B aircraft for the carriers. To date the UK has ordered just four F-35B aircraft. These have been delivered and are all being used in the US, three for training and the fourth as the UK trials aircraft. An answer to a written question in parliament placed in November stated that "A decision on Main Gate 4 for the Joint Strike Fighter programme is planned for the coming months." It seems that despite the first two squadrons to operate the F-35B being confirmed as 617 Squadron (RAF) and 899 NAS the government is yet to make a decision on ordering the aircraft. The issue of how many aircraft will be required and who will operate them raises interesting questions.

In 2010 when the RAF withdrew the Harrier it stated that there was no longer a role for the VTOL aircraft and that the Tornado was a more capable aircraft for their needs. The future strike aircraft for both the RAF and RN was at this stage the F-35, with the RAF operating the F-35A conventional aircraft and the RN, the F-35B STOVL variant. The thinking was that the aircraft would be operated as was the Harrier, with a Joint Force Lightning, with one command, basing and maintenance organisation presenting significant savings. However, current thinking is that the F-35B will now be the only variant acquired, with all aircraft available for deployment to the aircraft carriers. The question must now be asked why the RAF is to have a vested interest in what is now a capability which less than five years ago they said they no longer had a requirement for. Under Joint Force Harrier a pool of aircraft were operated by joint Light Blue (RAF) and Dark Blue (RN) personnel, with the aircraft deployed on either RAF or RN tasking as required. JFH should have worked, but in reality, the differing requirements of the RAF and RN meant that the aircraft were rarely available for RN operations - and when they were, aircraft tended to "meet" the carrier for a few weeks of training to keep aircrews current or to requalify pilots returning from the desert. If we are to look to the history books it will be seen that this is not a new issue. From the time the Royal Flying Corps and the Royal Naval Air Service merged in 1918 to become the Royal Air Force, the RN (and the Army) have had to argue the case for their own organic air power. The 1921 Balfour Report recognised the role the RAF could play in strategic operations and fighter defence and long range bombing were considered the preserve of the RAF, but it was to be a further three years before the Fleet Air Arm was formed - and even then it comprised flights of aircraft under the control of the RAF. The debate continued through to 1937 when the Inskip report finally conceded that the FAA should be placed under Admiralty control.

Over 75 years later, the same arguments are still being played out, but a decision is needed quickly - the carriers are nearing completion and attention must turn to acquiring aircraft, aircrews and handlers who will be able to deploy to the ship, integrate with the ship, and remain with the ship whenever it is at sea. To operate jet aircraft from such a large aircraft carrier takes months of training to achieve a

4

safe operating standard - and, more importantly, months of continuous flying operations at sea to maintain and hone those skills - this requires aircraft to remain with, and operate from, the carriers whenever they are at sea. It must remembered the RAF and the FAA are totally different in both requirements and ethos - being onboard a carrier for months at a time is not just about flying. The Fleet Air Arm are sailors who fly, rather than airmen who go to sea.

With the Type 45 build programme now complete attention is turning towards the Type 23 frigate replacement programme - the Type 26. Construction of the first vessel is intended to start around 2016 with a 2020 completion date. The whole programme is expected to complete around 2036 when the last Type 23 leaves service. However, there are potential issues which could hamper the smooth progress of this programme.

UK warship building is now vested in a single supplier, BAE Systems, which operates a monopoly of three shipbuilding yards in the UK, Govan and Scotstoun on the Clyde and Portsmouth. With the dearth of UK warship orders (the last major warships, the Queen Elizabeth class were ordered in 2007) it was obvious that there was going to be an overcapacity at UK yards. In 2005 the MoD signed a terms of Business Agreement with the contractors, guaranteeing a set amount of warship work through to 2020. That work could not sustain all three yards so changes would have to be made. In November 2013, BAE announced that all warship building would cease at Portsmouth and that its shipbuilding arm would centre on the Clyde and the MoD announced that the Type 26 build programme would be undertaken in Scotland. The elephant in the room, however, is that this year (2014) Scotland will hold a referendum to determine whether the country wants to become independent from the remaining UK. If the result is a yes vote for independence, then the Type 26 work will move from Scotland back to yards within the remaining UK - but this would then require either a massive injection of cash into long since closed yards to enable them to build complex warships again, or an international tender process to allow overseas shipyards to compete for the contract to build RN warships. The Government is taking a massive gamble in anticipation of a "No" vote by the people of Scotland.

In the interim, to tide the shipyards over until the Type 26 is ready to begin construction the MoD would have had to pay the contractor to keep the yards open - so rather than get nothing for their money, the MoD are to order three OPVs to an improved River design, despite repeating on several occasions throughout 2013 that the RN had no requirement for extra OPVs. The new OPVs will be 90m in length and have a flightdeck capable of landing a Merlin. Although no further details were given it was said in Parliament, in November 2013, that "the project will be subject to Main Gate approval in the coming months and, as is the standard practice with equipment projects, the final design, equipment fit and build programme will not finally be set until this main investment decision has been taken". It is expected that construction of the first of the three vessels will begin in 2014. It was expected that the ships will replace the earlier River class used for Fishery Protection, but that decision is not due to be made until the 2015 Defence review. It is to be hoped that these vessels can be funded as additional units and be deployed to provide an enduring presence in the Caribbean, Falklands, Mediterranean or off the Horn of Africa, releasing the hard pressed, and expensive, destroyers and frigates for more complex operational taking.

As part of the SDSR the MoD set up the Response Force Task Group, held at very high readiness to respond to unexpected global events. Since 2011 the group has deployed for exercises around the globe, centred on a large amphibious group and supported by RFAs. I have reservations about the concept of this strategy - to date, these high value units have deployed, often lacking the air defence or ASW assets you would expect to be needed to protect such ships. If the UK are really going to demonstrate such a capability, with annual deployments to prove the concept, surely the requirement should be for a fully rounded and representative task group to be deployed. My second issue is that its advertised tasking includes a diverse range of defence activities such as non-combatant evacuation operations, disaster relief, humanitarian aid or amphibious operations. The Type 45 destroyer DARING was, in November, diverted from Singapore to offer support to the Philippines in the wake of Typhoon Haiyan. Several days later, the carrier ILLUSTRIOUS was diverted to eventually relieve DARING. Given the scale of the disaster and the human suffering, why did the UK not deploy the entire RFTG comprising, ILLUSTRIOUS, BULWARK, MOUNTS BAY and LYME BAY, together with supporting RFAs and escorts, to the area? With their helicopters, landing craft, lift capacity, command and contral facilities and manpower, they are ideal vessels - and at the time already deployed in the Gulf region. If, as the government contends, these ships are held at very high readiness to respond to, among others, disaster relief and humanitarian aid, why were they not diverted from an exercise scenario to assist in a desperate real world situation?

Steve Bush
November 2013

SHIPS OF THE ROYAL NAVY
Pennant Numbers

Ship	Pennant Number	Page	Ship	Pennant Number	Page
Helicopter Carriers			**Submarines**		
ILLUSTRIOUS	R06	13	VANGUARD	S28	9
			VICTORIOUS	S29	9
Assault Ships			VIGILANT	S30	9
			VENGEANCE	S31	9
OCEAN	L12	14	TIRELESS	S88	12
ALBION *	L14	15	TORBAY	S90	12
BULWARK	L15	15	TRENCHANT	S91	12
			TALENT	S92	12
Destroyers			TRIUMPH	S93	12
			ASTUTE	S119	10
DARING	D32	16	AMBUSH	S120	10
DAUNTLESS	D33	16			
DIAMOND	D34	16	**Minehunters**		
DRAGON	D35	16			
DEFENDER	D36	16	LEDBURY	M30	20
DUNCAN	D37	16	CATTISTOCK	M31	20
			BROCKLESBY	M33	20
Frigates			MIDDLETON	M34	20
			CHIDDINGFOLD	M37	20
KENT	F78	18	ATHERSTONE	M38	20
PORTLAND	F79	18	HURWORTH	M39	20
SUTHERLAND	F81	18	QUORN	M41	20
SOMERSET	F82	18	PENZANCE	M106	22
ST ALBANS	F83	18	PEMBROKE	M107	22
LANCASTER	F229	18	GRIMSBY	M108	22
ARGYLL	F231	18	BANGOR	M109	22
IRON DUKE	F234	18	RAMSEY	M110	22
MONMOUTH	F235	18	BLYTH	M111	22
MONTROSE	F236	18	SHOREHAM	M112	22
WESTMINSTER	F237	19			
NORTHUMBERLAND	F238	19	**Patrol Craft**		
RICHMOND	F239	19			
			EXPRESS	P163	26

Ship	Pennant Number	Page	Ship	Pennant Number	Page
EXPLORER	P164	26	PUNCHER	P291	27
EXAMPLE	P165	26	CHARGER	P292	27
EXPLOIT	P167	26	RANGER	P293	27
CLYDE	P257	24	TRUMPETER	P294	27
ARCHER	P264	26			
BITER	P270	26	**Survey Ships & RN**		
SMITER	P272	26	**Manned Auxiliaries**		
PURSUER	P273	26			
TRACKER	P274	26	GLEANER	H86	30
RAIDER	P275	26	ECHO	H87	29
BLAZER	P279	26	ENTERPRISE	H88	29
DASHER	P280	26	SCOTT	H131	28
TYNE	P281	23	ENDURANCE	A171	32
SEVERN	P282	23	PROTECTOR	A173	31
MERSEY	P283	23			
SCIMITAR	P284	25	** Vessel is at extended readiness*		
SABRE	P285	25			

HMS Victorious

SUBMARINES
VANGUARD CLASS

Ship	Pennant Number	Completion Date	Builder
VANGUARD	S28	1992	VSEL
VICTORIOUS	S29	1994	VSEL
VIGILANT	S30	1997	VSEL
VENGEANCE	S31	1999	VSEL

Displacement 15,980 tons (dived) **Dimensions** 149.9m x 12.8m x 12m **Speed** 25 + dived **Armament** 16 Tubes for Trident 2 (D5) missiles, 4 Torpedo Tubes **Complement** 135

Notes

After the first successful UK D5 missile firing in May '94 the first operational patrol was carried out in early '95 and a patrol has been constantly maintained ever since. The UK's Trident missiles have been de-targeted since 1994, and the submarine on deterrent patrol is normally at several days notice to fire her missiles. VENGEANCE, the final submarine to enter the refit cycle, arrived at Devonport on 2 March 2012. Due to delays in the Successor submarine programme, the service life of the Vanguard class has been extended to beyond 2028 while at the same time reducing the number of operational missiles on each submarine to just eight. To achieve this five year extension three additional Long Overhaul Periods (LOPs) will be required, at Devonport, costing around £1.3 billion between 2014 and 2024.

HMS Astute (with dry deck shelter)

ASTUTE CLASS

Ship	Pennant Number	Completion Date	Builder
ASTUTE	S119	2009	BAe Submarine Solutions
AMBUSH	S120	2012	BAe Submarine Solutions
ARTFUL	S121	Building	BAe Submarine Solutions
AUDACIOUS	S122	Building	BAe Submarine Solutions
ANSON	S123	Building	BAe Submarine Solutions
AGAMEMNON	S124	Planned	BAe Submarine Solutions
AJAX	S125	Planned	BAe Submarine Solutions

Displacement 7,400 tonnes (7,800 dived) **Dimensions** 97m x 11.2m x 9.5m **Speed** 29+ dived **Armament** 6 Torpedo Tubes; Spearfish torpedoes; Tomahawk cruise missiles for a payload of 38 weapons **Complement** 98 (Accommodation for 12 Officers and 97 Ratings)

Notes

Ordered in 1997, the Astute class will replace the Trafalgar class in RN service. AMBUSH was commissioned on 1 March 2013, having arrived at Faslane on 19 September 2012. The third boat ARTFUL was formally named on 20 September 2013 and is due to be rolled out of Devonshire Dock Hall and launched in early 2014. Sea trials should start about 12 months later. The hull of AUDACIOUS is nearing completion and commissioning work should be underway in 2014. All major fabrications for ANSON are now complete and awaiting assembly. The keel ring for the sixth submarine, AGAMEMNON, was ceremonially laid down on 18 July. The seventh submarine, AJAX, has been confirmed, but not yet ordered.

The Astute class is designed to fulfil a range of key strategic and tactical roles including anti-ship and anti-submarine operations, surveillance and intelligence gathering and support for land forces. Each boat will have a lock in lock out capability, enabling swimmers to leave the submarine while dived. This capability is in addition to the Chalfont dry deck hangar which can be fitted to the aft casing and designed to hold a swimmer delivery vehicle for stand off insertion.

The fourth boat, AUDACIOUS, is the first to benefit from a so-called Design for Cost Reduction initiative, a redesign activity pursued by BAE Systems, the MoD and its key suppliers to ensure the affordability of later boats, addressing both the platform and combat system. As well as re-engineering certain parts of the original design, there was a move to commercial-off-the-shelf systems for some of the combat system equipments.

The planned in-service dates for the remainder of the Astute class boats are: ARTFUL (2015); AUDACIOUS (2018); ANSON (2020); AGAMEMNON (2022) and AJAX (2024).

HMS Tireless

TRAFALGAR CLASS

Ship	Pennant Number	Completion Date	Builder
TIRELESS	S88	1985	Vickers
TORBAY	S90	1986	Vickers
TRENCHANT	S91	1989	Vickers
TALENT	S92	1990	Vickers
TRIUMPH	S93	1991	Vickers

Displacement 4,500 tons 5,200 tons dived **Dimensions** 85.4m x 9.8m x 9.5m **Speed** 30+ dived **Armament** 5 Torpedo Tubes; Spearfish torpedoes; Tomahawk cruise missiles for a payload of 24 weapons **Complement** 130

Notes

TORBAY, TALENT, TRENCHANT and TRIUMPH have undergone upgrade and received Type 2076 Sonar. In September 2013 TRENCHANT began a substantial two year Revalidation and Assisted Maintenance Period at Devonport, having returned, in May, from a record breaking 335 day patrol, including 267 days east of Suez. Beginning in 2014 the final four submarines are to undergo a communications package upgrade to overcome obsolescence issues. With delays to the Astute class decommissioning dates for the remaining T class have been extended. As at July 2013 proposed decommissioning dates are TIRELESS (2014); TORBAY (2017); TRENCHANT (2019); TALENT (2021) and TRIUMPH (2022).

LANDING PLATFORM HELICOPTER (LPH)

INVINCIBLE CLASS

Ship	Pennant Number	Completion Date	Builder
ILLUSTRIOUS	R06	1982	Swan Hunter

Displacement 22,500 tonnes **Dimensions** 210m x 36m x 6.5m **Speed** 28 knots **Armament** 2 - 20mm guns, 3 Goalkeeper **Aircraft** Tailored Air Group (Merlin, Sea King, Chinook, Apache as required) **Complement** 726 + 384 Air Group (600 troops)

Notes

The last of three Invincible class aircraft carriers in service, ILLUSTRIOUS now serves in the LPH role. She is scheduled to be withdrawn from service in 2014 when OCEAN completes her refit. In 2012 the MoD stated their wish that ILLUSTRIOUS, on decommissioning, should be preserved. The MoD are keen to seek innovative proposals from a range of organisations, including private sector companies, charities and trusts. In 2013 the MoD Disposal Services Authority (DSA) launched a competition seeking innovative re-use bids to retain the ship in the UK, with part or all of it developed for heritage purposes. Organisations would be expected to put forward 'mature and viable proposals, in keeping with the role and history of the Invincible class of ships'.

HMS Ocean

OCEAN

Ship	Pennant Number	Completion Date	Builder
OCEAN	L12	1998	Kvaerner

Displacement 22,500 tonnes **Dimensions** 203.8m x 35m x 6.6m **Speed** 17 knots **Armament** 3 x Phalanx, 4 x 30mm ASC guns, 4 x Minigun **Aircraft** Tailored Air Group (Merlin, Sea King, Chinook, Apache as required) **Complement** Ship 285, Squadrons 206 (maximum 1275 including Royal Marines)

Notes

Can carry 12 Sea King and 6 Lynx helicopters. RAF Chinook helicopters are normally carried as an integral part of the ship's air group, but they are unable to be stowed below decks. Modified with two 50m blisters attached to the hull at the waterline below the after chine to improve safety margins while deploying LCVPs from the after davits. Vessel is somewhat constrained by her slow speed. Many improvements have been made to her including accomodation for both crew and embarked Royal Marines; advanced communications facilities; a better weapon defence system and an upgrade to the ship's aviation support facilities to improve support to helicopter operations including the Apache attack helicopter. In July 2013 the ship was moved from dry-dock, a major milestone in her refit, scheduled to finish in 2014. Major upgrades have included the installation of Type 997 (Artisan) radar and the replacing of the 20mm guns by four 30mm Automated Small Calibre gun systems.

HMS Bulwark

LANDING PLATFORM DOCK (LPD)

ALBION CLASS

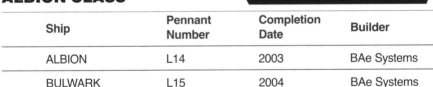

Ship	Pennant Number	Completion Date	Builder
ALBION	L14	2003	BAe Systems
BULWARK	L15	2004	BAe Systems

Displacement 18,500 tons, 21,500 tons (flooded) **Dimensions** 176m x 25.6m x 7.1m
Speed 18 knots **Armament** 2 x CIWS, 2 x 20mm guns (single) **Complement** 325
Military Lift 303 troops, with an overload capacity of a further 405

Notes

Vehicle deck capacity for up to six Challenger 2 tanks or around 30 armoured all-terrain
tracked vehicles. Floodable well dock able to take four utility landing craft. Four smaller
landing craft carried on davits. Two-spot flight deck able to take medium support helicopters
and stow a third. Flightdeck allows the simultaneous operation of two Chinook helicopters.
These vessels do not have a hangar but have equipment needed to support aircraft operations. Only one of the class remains operational at this time. BULWARK assumed the role
of fleet flagship in October 2011. In 2012 ALBION entered a 33-month period of extended
readiness during which time she provided training for Landing Craft Davit operations. In
2014 she will undergo a regeneration refit and rejoin the fleet in 2016.

HMS Duncan

DESTROYERS
DARING CLASS
(Type 45)

Ship	Pennant Number	Completion Date	Builder
DARING	D32	2008	BVT Surface Fleet
DAUNTLESS	D33	2008	BVT Surface Fleet
DIAMOND	D34	2009	BVT Surface Fleet
DRAGON	D35	2011	BVT Surface Fleet
DEFENDER	D36	2012	BVT Surface Fleet
DUNCAN	D37	2013	BVT Surface Fleet

Displacement 7,350 tons **Dimensions** 152.4m x 21.2m x 5.7m **Speed** 29 knots **Armament** 1 - 4.5-inch gun, Sea Viper missile system comprising Sylver VLS with combination of up to 48 Aster 15 and Aster 30 missiles, 2 x Vulcan Phalanx (fitted as required) **Aircraft** Lynx or Merlin **Complement** 190 (with space for 235)

Notes

Originally to have been a class of "up to" 12 ships this was reduced to just six. The bow sections, funnels and masts were built at Portsmouth and then transported by barge to Govan where final assembly and fitting out took place. DEFENDER arrived at Portsmouth for the first time on 25 July 2012 and, following trials, was accepted into the fleet in March 2013. Following sea training she will be ready to deploy in 2014. The final vessel, DUNCAN, was commissioned on 26 September 2013, bringing to an end the Type 45 build programme. She will continue with sea trials throughout 2014.

DRAGON is the first of the batch two destroyers, which include upgrades to systems onboard in line with technological developments.

It is intended that the Harpoon missile systems removed from the decommissioned Type 22 frigates will be fitted to four of the Type 45 destroyers.

Royal Navy destroyer strength is now vested in just six Type 45s, as the final Type 42, EDINBURGH, was decommissioned on 6 June 2013, bringing to an end 38 years of Type 42 operations in the Royal Navy.

HMS Iron Duke (with Artisan radar)

FRIGATES
DUKE CLASS (Type 23)

Ship	Pennant Number	Completion Date	Builder
KENT	F78	2000	Yarrow
PORTLAND	F79	2000	Yarrow
SUTHERLAND	F81	1997	Yarrow
SOMERSET	F82	1996	Yarrow
ST ALBANS	F83	2001	Yarrow
LANCASTER	F229	1991	Yarrow
ARGYLL	F231	1991	Yarrow
IRON DUKE	F234	1992	Yarrow
MONMOUTH	F235	1993	Yarrow
MONTROSE	F236	1993	Yarrow

Ship	Pennant Number	Completion Date	Builder
WESTMINSTER	F237	1993	Swan Hunter
NORTHUMBERLAND	F238	1994	Swan Hunter
RICHMOND	F239	1994	Swan Hunter

Displacement 4,900 tonnes **Dimensions** 133m x 16.1m x 5m **Speed** 28 knots **Armament** Harpoon & Seawolf missile systems: 1 - 4.5-inch gun, 2 - single 30mm guns, 4 - 2 twin, magazine launched, Torpedo Tubes, Lynx or Merlin helicopter **Complement** 185

Notes

Now the sole class of frigate in RN service, the ships incorporate 'Stealth' technology to minimise magnetic, radar, acoustic and infra-red signatures. Gas turbine and diesel electric propulsion. All ships are now fitted with the Mk 8 Mod 1 4.5-inch gun. Type 2087 Sonar is to be fitted in only 9 of the remaining 13 of the class (ARGYLL, MONTROSE, MONMOUTH and IRON DUKE will not receive the upgrade). Both SOMERSET and PORTLAND returned to the fleet in 2013 following refit periods

In August 2008 the MoD announced that the Type 996 surveillance and target indication radar was to be replaced by the ARTISAN 3D Medium Range Radar (now designated Type 997) under a £100 million contract covering demonstration, manufacturing, delivery and the first 10 years of in-service support. The ARTISAN 3D (Advanced Radar Target Indication Situational Awareness and Navigation) is a modular open architecture maritime radar system designed to deal with complex littoral environments. It is being incrementally installed between 2011 and 2015. IRON DUKE recieved its new radar during a refit period that commenced in March 2012, re-entering sevice in 2013.

The Seawolf missile system is expected to reach the end of its service life around 2018 and will be replaced by the Sea Ceptor between 2015-2021.

Under current plans ships are scheduled to decommission as follows: ARGYLL 2023; LANCASTER 2024; IRON DUKE 2025; MONMOUTH 2026; MONTROSE 2027; WESTMINSTER 2028; NORTHUMBERLAND 2029 ; RICHMOND 2030; SOMERSET 2031; SUTHERLAND 2033; KENT 2034; PORTLAND 2035 and ST. ALBANS 2036.

HMS Ledbury

MINE COUNTERMEASURES SHIPS (MCMV)
HUNT CLASS

Ship	Pennant Number	Completion Date	Builder
LEDBURY	M30	1981	Vosper T.
CATTISTOCK	M31	1982	Vosper T.
BROCKLESBY	M33	1983	Vosper T.
MIDDLETON	M34	1984	Yarrow
CHIDDINGFOLD	M37	1984	Vosper T.
ATHERSTONE	M38	1987	Vosper T.
HURWORTH	M39	1985	Vosper T.
QUORN	M41	1989	Vosper T.

Displacement 750 tonnes **Dimensions** 60m x 10.5m x 3.4m **Speed** 15 knots **Armament** 1 x 30mm + 2 x Miniguns **Complement** 45

Notes

The largest warships ever built of glass reinforced plastic. Their cost (£35m each) has dictated the size of the class. Very sophisticated ships - and lively seaboats! All are based at Portsmouth as the Second Mine Countermeasures Squadron (MCM2).

BAE Systems has been awarded a six-year contract worth £15m to replace the propulsion systems on these ships, with the work to be carried out at Portsmouth. The first new propulsion system, comprising two Caterpillar C32 engines (replacing the older Napier Deltics) has been installed on board CHIDDINGFOLD which returned to service in 2013. Upgrades to the remaining seven ships will take place during planned ship docking periods up to 2016. The re-propulsion project will involve the installation of new engines, gearboxes, bow thruster systems, propellers and machinery control systems.

LEDBURY to decommission in 2019, CATTISTOCK, BROCKLESBY, CHIDDINGFOLD and MIDDLETON 2020, HURWORTH and ATHERSTONE 2022 and QUORN 2023. In order to keep up the overseas deployment tempo, crews are swapped between ships. ATHERSTONE and QUORN are forward deployed to the Gulf.

In 2013 the 9th MCM Squadron was stood up at Bahrain, comprising those vessels deployed to the Gulf in support of mine countermeasures operations. Those ships will be identified by a squadron funnel emblem depicting a traditional dhow, resurrecting the identity of the Ton class vessels deployed to the Gulf in the 1960s and 1970s as 9th MSS and latterly 9th MCMS

HMS Pembroke

SANDOWN CLASS

Ship	Pennant Number	Completion Date	Builder
PENZANCE	M106	1998	Vosper T.
PEMBROKE	M107	1998	Vosper T.
GRIMSBY	M108	1999	Vosper T.
BANGOR	M109	2000	Vosper T.
RAMSEY	M110	2000	Vosper T.
BLYTH	M111	2001	Vosper T.
SHOREHAM	M112	2001	Vosper T.

Displacement 600 tons **Dimensions** 52.5m x 109.m x 2m **Speed** 13 knots
Armament 1 - 30mm gun; 2 x Miniguns; 3 x GPMG **Complement** 34

Notes

A class dedicated to a single mine hunting role. Propulsion is by vectored thrust and
bow thrusters. All are based at Faslane as the First Mine Countermeasures Squadron
(MCM1). The ships are manned by eight numbered crews which are rotated throughout the squadron allowing deployed vessels to remain on station for extended periods.
RAMSEY and SHOREHAM are forward deployed to the Gulf.

HMS Tyne

PATROL VESSELS
RIVER CLASS

Ship	Pennant Number	Completion Date	Builder
TYNE	P281	2002	Vosper T.
SEVERN	P282	2003	Vosper T.
MERSEY	P283	2003	Vosper T.

Displacement 1,677 tonnes **Dimensions** 79.5m x 13.6m x 3.8m **Speed** 20+ knots
Armament 1 x 20mm; 2 x GPMG **Complement** 48

Notes

Ordered on 8 May 2001, the deal was unusual in that the ships were leased from Vospers (VT) for five years under a £60 million contract. The lease arrangement appeared to have been a success with VT meeting their commitment of having the ships available for over 300 days a year. In January 2007 a £52 million lease-contract extension was awarded extending their RN service to the end of 2013. In September 2012, rather than face having to pay more to rent the vessels – £7m a year for all three – Whitehall signed a £39m contract to buy the ships outright, keeping them in service with the RN for the next ten years. The River class are now the only RN ships permanently conducting Fishery Protection patrols in the waters around England, Wales and Northern Ireland. In November 2013 it was announced that a further three OPVs were to be built for the RN. They will be larger and have a flightdeck able to operate a Merlin helicopter. it is probable that the design will be to the Improved River class design, similar to the ships delivered to the Brazilian Navy.

HMS Clyde

BATCH II RIVER CLASS

Ship	Pennant Number	Completion Date	Builder
CLYDE	P257	2006	VT Shipbuilding

Displacement 1,847 tonnes **Dimensions** 81.5m x 13.6m x 4.15m **Speed** 19 knots (full load) 21 knots (sprint) **Aircraft** Flight Deck to take Lynx, Sea King or Merlin Helicopter **Armament** 1 - 30mm gun; 5 x GPMG; 2 x Minigun **Complement** 36 (space for additional 20 personnel - see note)

Notes

Designed to carry out patrol duties around the Falkland Islands and their dependencies, the ship is able to accommodate a single helicopter up to Merlin size. She deployed to the Falklands in August 2007. CLYDE's more modern design has enabled her to remain on task in the South Atlantic until later this year. Like the previous River class, she had been leased from BAE Systems, for a period of five years. In July 2011 it was announced that BAE Systems had been awarded a six-year contract extension to deliver support services to the ship until 2018. The annual cost to the public purse of operating the ship is £3.5 million.

CLYDE is able to embark a Military Force of up to 110 personnel (the size of the Roulement Infantry Company (RIC)) and move them around the Falkland Islands, inserting them at will.

HMS Scimitar

SCIMITAR CLASS

Ship	Pennant Number	Completion Date	Builder
SCIMITAR	P284	1988	Halmatic
SABRE	P285	1988	Halmatic

Displacement 18.5 tons   **Dimensions** 16m x 4.7m x 1.4m   **Speed** 27+ knots
Armament 2 x GPMG **Complement** 4

Notes

Purpose built in 1988 for counter terrorism duties on Lough Neagh, Northern Ireland. Operated in anonimity as GREYFOX and GREYWOLF until withdrawn from service in 2002 and transferred to Gibraltar to join the Royal Navy Gibraltar Squadron (RNGS). The Squadron comprises the two Scimitar-class patrol boats, 21 personnel, and three Pacific rigid-hulled inflatable boats. RNGS provides Force Protection to visiting coalition warships, maritime security patrols within British Gibraltar Territorial Waters and supports a variety of operations within the Joint Operating Area. In recent months the craft have been facing increasingly provocative stand-offs with their Spanish counterparts in the Guardia Civil as Spain tries to assert its influence over what it views as disputed waters in the Bay of Gibraltar.

HMS Explorer

COASTAL TRAINING CRAFT
P2000 CLASS

Ship	Pennant Number	Completion Date	Builder
EXPRESS	P163	1988	Vosper T.
EXPLORER	P164	1985	Watercraft
EXAMPLE	P165	1985	Watercraft
EXPLOIT	P167	1988	Vosper T.
ARCHER	P264	1985	Watercraft
BITER	P270	1985	Watercraft
SMITER	P272	1986	Watercraft
PURSUER	P273	1988	Vosper T.
TRACKER	P274	1998	Ailsa Troon
RAIDER	P275	1998	Ailsa Troon
BLAZER	P279	1988	Vosper T.
DASHER	P280	1988	Vosper T.

Ship	Pennant Number	Completion Date	Builder
PUNCHER	P291	1988	Vosper T.
CHARGER	P292	1988	Vosper T.
RANGER	P293	1988	Vosper T.
TRUMPETER	P294	1988	Vosper T.

Displacement 54 tonnes **Dimensions** 20m x 5.8m x 1.9m **Speed** 20 knots **Armament** 3 x GPMG (Faslane based vessels) **Complement** 5 (with accommodation for up to 12 undergraduates).

Notes

Fourteen P2000 craft form the First Patrol Boat Squadron, whose primary role is to support the University Royal Naval Units (URNU) but also contribute to a wide range of Fleet tasking. Commodore Britannia Royal Naval College has overall responsibility for the URNUs whose role is to educate and inform a wide spectrum of high calibre undergraduates. Training is conducted one evening a week in shore units at or near the University and at sea, over the weekends and during the vacations, by a dedicated patrol craft. Vessels are assigned to the following URNUs: ARCHER (East Scotland); BITER (Manchester & Salford); BLAZER (Southampton); CHARGER (Liverpool); DASHER (Bristol); EXAMPLE (Northumbria); EXPLOIT (Birmingham); EXPLORER (Yorkshire); EXPRESS (Wales); PUNCHER (London); PURSUER (Glasgow & Strathclyde); RANGER (Sussex); SMITER (Oxford); TRUMPETER (Cambridge). On 28 September 2012, ARCHER was relocated from Aberdeen to Leith, a move that is hoped will offer greater training opportunities in the more sheltered waters of the Firth of Forth.

The last two vessels built, RAIDER and TRACKER, have a higher top speed of 24 knots as they are fitted with two MTU V12 diesels. They now comprise the Faslane Patrol Boat Squadron. Formed in March 2010, the Squadron provides Force Protection in and around Faslane, Scotland. Initially PURSUER and DASHER were relocated to HMNB Clyde from Cyprus in April 2010, arriving at their new home on 6 May that year. They were replaced by RAIDER and TRACKER in September 2012. They are fully-fledged armed patrol boats. Fitted with Kevlar armour and able to mount three 7.62mm General Purpose Machine Guns (GPMG) they are part of a growing Force Protection cadre based at Faslane to protect the UKs nuclear deterrent. These two vessels are fully engaged in FP duties and do not undertake university training.

HMS Scott

SURVEY SHIPS
SCOTT CLASS

Ship	Pennant Number	Completion Date	Builder
SCOTT	H 131	1997	Appledore

Displacement 13,300 tonnes **Dimensions** 131.5m x 21.5m x 9m **Speed** 17 knots
Complement 63 (42 embarked at any one time)

Notes

Designed to commercial standards SCOTT provides the RN with a deep bathymetric capability off the continental shelf. Fitted with a modern multi-beam sonar suite she can conduct mapping of the ocean floor worldwide. She carries a mixture of the latest UK and US survey equipment. She operates a three watch system whereby the vessel is run by 42 of her ship's company of 63 - with the remainder on leave. Each crew member works 75 days in the ship before having 30 days off, allowing her to spend more than 300 days at sea in a year. Extensive use of commercial lean manning methods including unmanned machinery spaces, fixed fire fighting systems and extensive machinery and safety surveillance technology. Her hull is Ice class 1A: Ships with such structure, engine output and other properties are capable of navigating in difficult ice conditions, but only with the assistance of icebreakers. In 2013 Babcock won a five year contract from the MoD to provide through life engineering support to the ship. In October 2013 SCOTT began a 7-month drydocking and upgrade period at Devonport, during which she will receive a number of upgrades and improvements, including a new sewage treatment plant and new lifeboat davits, as well as a new uninterrupted power supply to the ship's sonar suite.

HMS Enterprise

ECHO CLASS

Ship	Pennant Number	Completion Date	Builder
ECHO	H 87	2002	Appledore
ENTERPRISE	H 88	2003	Appledore

Displacement 3,500 tonnes **Dimensions** 90m x 16.8m x 5.5.m **Speed** 15 knots
Armament 2 x 20mm **Complement** 49 (with accommodation for 81)

Notes

In June 2000, a £130 million order was placed with prime contractor Vosper Thornycroft to build and maintain, over a 25 year period, these two new Survey Vessels Hydrographic Oceanographic (SVHO). Both vessels were built by sub-contractor Appledore Shipbuilding Limited. They have a secondary role as mine countermeasures HQ ships. The total ship's company is 72, with 48 personnel onboard at any one time working a cycle of 75 days on, 30 days off, allowing the ships to be operationally available for 330 days a year. Utilizing a diesel electric propulsion system, they have three main generators. They are the first RN ships to be fitted with Azimuth pod thrusters in place of the more normal shaft and propellor. Each ship carries a named survey launch, SAPPHIRE (ECHO) and SPITFIRE (ENTERPRISE). SPITFIRE is a new design 9m SMB powered by two 6-cylinder diesels linked to jet propulsion units. It is equipped with side scan sonar and both multi-beam and single beam echo sounders. In September 2013 ENTERPRISE emerged from drydock following a maintenance period at Falmouth. Following work-up she will deploy in 2014. In June 2013 ECHO sailed for an eighteen month deployment.

HMS Gleaner

INSHORE SURVEY VESSEL

Ship	Pennant Number	Completion Date	Builder
GLEANER	H86	1983	Emsworth

Displacement 26 tons **Dimensions** 14.8m x 4.7m x 1.6m **Speed** 14 knots
Complement 8

Notes

Small inshore survey craft used for the collection of data from the shallowest inshore waters. She uses multibeam and sidescan sonar to collect bathymetry and seabed texture data and compile an accurate and detailed picture of the seabed. She was scheduled to decommission in 2007, but she emerged, in 2008, from a Service Life Extension Programme, which will enable her to remain in service for a further 10 years. She carries the prefix Her Majesty's Survey Motor Launch or HMSML.

Four small survey boats, NESBITT, PAT BARTON, COOK and OWEN are attached to the Hydrographic School at Devonport.

HMS Protector

ICE PATROL SHIPS
PROTECTOR

Ship	Pennant Number	Completion Date	Builder
PROTECTOR	A173	2001	Havyard Leirvik (Norway)

Displacement 4,985 tons **Dimensions** 89.7m x 18m x 7.25m **Speed** 15 knots
Armament Miniguns; GPMGs **Complement** 88

Notes

The ice-breaker MV POLARBJORN was initially leased, in June 2011, on a three-year contract from the Norwegian company GC Rieber Shipping as a temporary replacement for the damaged ENDURANCE and commissioned as PROTECTOR. In 2013 it was announced that the ship had been bought by the MoD and that she would be a permanent replacement for ENDURANCE. Although the ship has a flight deck, there is no hangar, so she will be unable to deploy with an embarked helicopter. She operates the Survey Motor Boat JAMES CAIRD IV and the 8.5 metre Rigid Work Boat TERRA NOVA. She can also deploy two Pacific 22 RIBs (NIMROD and AURORA). She also deploys with three BV206 all terrain vehicles and four quadbikes and trailers to assist in moving stores and equipment. On 17 October 2013 she sailed from Portsmouth, for the last time, for a double deployment to Antarctica. The ship will stay in the region for two consecutive deployments, returning to her new home at Devonport Naval Base in Spring 2015, where she will be based with the rest of the Hydrographic fleet.

HMS Endurance

ENDURANCE

Ship	Pennant Number	Completion Date	Builder
ENDURANCE	A171	1990	Ulstein-Hatlo

Displacement 5,129 tons **Dimensions** 91m x 17.9m x 6.5m **Speed** 14.9 knots
Armament Small arms **Aircraft** 2 Lynx **Complement** 116

Notes

Chartered for only 7 months in late 1991 to replace the older vessel of the same name. Originally M/V POLAR CIRCLE, renamed HMS POLAR CIRCLE (A176) and then purchased by MoD(N) and renamed again in October 1992 to current name. Historically spent 4-6 months each year in the South Atlantic supporting the British Antarctic Survey. Following a flooding incident off Chile in 2008 she was returned to the UK aboard a heavylift ship in April 2009. She has remained at Portsmouth ever since.

In 2013 it was announced that PROTECTOR had been bought as a permanent replacement and that ENDURANCE would be withdrawn from service in 2015. The wording of the announcement was odd considering that the ship has been deteriorating at Portsmouth since being returned in 2009 and could never be considered as being "in service".

ROYAL MARINE CRAFT

In August 2013 the Royal Marines concentrated their various assault and landing craft at a newly built facility, housed at Devonport Naval Base. RM Tamar, as it is now known, is home to the RMs Landing Craft, Hovercraft and other vessels when not required for deployment, either onboard the assault ships, or independently.

Based at RM Tamar is 1 Assault Group Royal Marines (1 AGRM), the lead for amphibious warfare and Royal Navy board and search training. The group is tasked with training and developing core amphibious and surface assault skills and equipment, including the provision of operational support for the Ministry of Defence.

1 AGRM is responsible for 4 subordinate units which deliver the vast spectrum of training and operations required in delivering amphibious and surface assault capability of the Royal Navy and Royal Marines.

10 (Landing Craft) Training Squadron - Responsible for delivering landing craftsmen training as well as small boats, engineering and assault navigation training.

11 Amphibious Trials and Training Squadron (Instow, North Devon) - Delivering training that covers the area between the craft and the beachhead. The Instow squadron also conducts the trials and testing of future craft.

The Royal Navy School of Board and Search at HMS Raleigh in Torpoint trains both individuals and ship's boarding teams to conduct the full range of boarding operations that is required by the Naval Service.

In addition, 1AGRM is also tasked with parenting the Assault Squadrons of the Royal Marines (ASRMs) and their Landing Craft detachments which are assigned to the amphibious assault ships. These ASRMs provide the landing craft and therefore the fighting capability for the RN's Amphibious Ships, OCEAN (9 ASRM); ALBION (6 ASRM - currently disbanded and operated as 6 Ops Sqn until ALBION returns to service) and BULWARK (4 ASRM).

43 Commando Fleet Protection Group Royal Marines (43 Cdo FP Gp RM) is based at HM Naval Base Clyde near Helensburgh on the West Coast of Scotland. Formerly Comacchio Group it was renamed in April 2012 and, together with 539 ASRM, became part of 3 Commando Brigade. The Group's core task is to provide military support to undertake final denial of access to nuclear weapons in addition to supporting the multi-agency force that protects nuclear weapons convoys. Additionally, specially trained teams are deployed at short notice to conduct tasks in support of the RN worldwide. Tasks have ranged from Force Protection, to conducting non-compliant boarding operations and counter-piracy operations.

Rona

ISLAND CLASS PATROL VESSELS

Ship	Pennant Number	Launch Date	Builder
RONA	-	2009	Holyhead Marine
MULL	-	2010	Holyhead Marine

Displacement 19.9 tonnes   **Dimensions** 14.9m x 4.1m x 0.9m   **Speed** 33 knots
Armament 4 x GPMG   **Complement**

Notes

Originally units of a class of five launches delivered to the Ministry of Defence Police, RONA and MULL were transferred to 43 Commando Fleet Protection Group Royal Marines for operation on the Clyde to escort high value units. The vessels were returned to Holyhead Marine where they were modified in December 2012 and January 2013 respectvely. As well as major reworking of their upper decks, the vessels were fitted with three new weapon mounts, enhanced protection for coxswains and crew, as well as an enhanced communications package.

LCU Mk10 9737

LCU Mk10

Ship	Pennant Number	Parent Unit	Builder
9730	P1	10 Trg Sqn, TAMAR	Ailsa, Troon
9731	P2	11 ATT Sqn, INSTOW	Ailsa, Troon
9732	A1	6 Ops Sqn, TAMAR	BAE Systems
9733	B2	HMS BULWARK	BAE Systems
9734	A2	10 Trg Sqn, TAMAR	BAE Systems
9735	A3	HMS BULWARK	BAE Systems
9736	A4	HMS BULWARK	BAE Systems
9737	B1	HMS BULWARK	BAE Systems
9738	B3	6 Ops Sqn, TAMAR	BAE Systems
9739	FJ	10 Trg Sqn, TAMAR	BAE Systems

Displacement 240 tonnes **Dimensions** 29.82m x 7.7m x 1.70m **Speed** 8.5 knots **Armament** 2 x GPMG **Complement** 7

Notes

Ro-Ro style landing craft designed to operate from the Albion class LPDs or Landing Ship Dock Auxiliary (LSD(A)). Ordered in 1998 from Ailsa Troon. The first two were delivered in 1999 with the final vessels being accepted into service in 2003. The remainder were built by BAE Systems at Govan. Capable of lifting one Main Battle Tank or four lighter vehicles. Capacity for 100 fully equipped troops. With a range of around 600 nautical miles – more if auxiliary tanks are added – is designed to operate independently for 14 days with its seven man Royal Marine crew in both arctic and tropical climates. All the crew members have bunk accommodation and there is a galley and store rooms.

The MOD has trialled the PACSCAT (Partial Air Cushion Supported Catamaran), a high-speed landing craft developed by Qinetiq. Between August and December 2010, the craft was put through its paces at Instow in North Devon and in Scottish waters with ALBION. Similar in dimensions to the LCU Mk10 the craft is entirely constructed out of aluminium and is designed to offer the triple benefits of speed, manoeuvrability and payload capacity. It is 30 metres in length, just under eight metres in width and is capable of carrying loads weighing up to 55 tonnes. Propulsion was provided by a pair of MJP water jets powered by MTU-made diesel engines and during trials the craft demonstrated speeds in excess of 30 knots. With trials complete, the craft is now being advertised for sale.

LCVP Mk5B 0204

LCVP Mk5A/5B

Ship	Pennant Number	Parent Unit	Builder
Mk5A			
9707	-	10 Trg Sqn, TAMAR	Babcock Marine
9675	-	10 Trg Sqn, TAMAR	Vosper T.
9676	-	10 Trg Sqn, TAMAR	Vosper T.
Mk5B			
0202	A8	539 ASRM, TAMAR	Babcock Marine
0203	A6	HMS OCEAN	Babcock Marine
0204	A7	539 ASRM, TAMAR	Babcock Marine
0205	A5	10 Trg Sqn, TAMAR	Babcock Marine
0338	T6	11 ATT Sqn, INSTOW	Babcock Marine

Ship	Pennant Number	Parent Unit	Builder
0339	P6	10 Trg Sqn, TAMAR	Babcock Marine
0340	P7	HMS OCEAN	Babcock Marine
0341	P4	10 Trg Sqn, TAMAR	Babcock Marine
0344	NM	HMS BULWARK	Babcock Marine
0345	N2	HMS BULWARK	Babcock Marine
0346	N3	HMS OCEAN	Babcock Marine
0347	N4	HMS OCEAN	Babcock Marine
0353	B5	539 ASRM, TAMAR	Babcock Marine
0354	B6	539 ASRM, TAMAR	Babcock Marine
0355	B7	HMS BULWARK	Babcock Marine
0356	B8	HMS BULWARK	Babcock Marine

Displacement 24 tonnes **Dimensions** 15.70m x 3.5m x 0.90m **Speed** 25 knots **Armament** 2 x GPMG **Complement** 3

Notes

First one ordered in 1995 from Vosper Thornycroft and handed over in 1996. A further four were delivered in December 1996 to operate from OCEAN, with two more for training at RM Poole ordered in 1998. A further 16 were ordered from Babcock in 2001 with the final vessels being accepted into service in 2004. The Mk 5 can lift 8 tonnes of stores or a mix of 2 tonnes and 35 troops. These vessels have a greater range, lift and speed than the Mk4s which they replaced. The primary role is the landing of vehicles, personnel and equipment onto potentially hostile shores. The secondary role is a general purpose support craft both between ships and ship to shore. The craft is capable of performing its normal duties in conditions up to sea state 4 and run for cover up to sea state 5. Mk5As 9473, 9673, 9674 and 9708 have been disposed of.

Griffon 2400TD

4 GRIFFON 2400TD LCAC

Ship	Pennant Number	Completion Date	Builder
C23	-	2010	Griffon
C24	-	2010	Griffon
C25	-	2010	Griffon
C26	-	2010	Griffon

G.R.T. 6.8 tons **Dimensions** 13.4m x 6.8m **Speed** 45 knots **Range** 300 nm **Armament** 1 x GPMG **Complement** 2 Crew; 16 fully-equipped marines.

Notes

Operated by 539 Assault Squadron, the 2400TD offers greater payload, performance and obstacle clearance than the earlier 2000 TD craft. Centre sections of the cabin roof can be removed in order to embark two one-tonne NATO pallets. They can be transported on a standard low loader truck or in the hold of a C-130 Hercules aircraft. They can also operate directly from the well-deck of RN amphibious ships. They are equipped with a 7.62mm General Purpose Machine Gun, HF and VHF radios, radar, GPS, ballistic protection and a variety of specialised equipment. All four entered service by the end of 2010.

OFFSHORE RAIDING CRAFT

The Royal Marines operate two versions of the Offshore Raiding Craft (ORC), the Troop Carrying Variant (TCV) and Fire Support Variant (FSV). The ORC is an air portable surface manoeuvre craft designed for the rapid deployment of 8 fully equipped troops and 2 crew from over the horizon (30 miles) ship to shore and vice versa. They provide rapid movement of troops in coastal, estuarine, riverine and inland waters. Specifications: Weight: 3.6 tonnes - Length: 9.1m - Speed: 36 kts - Capacity: 2 Crew + 8 fully equipped troops.

RIGID RAIDING CRAFT

The Royal Marines operate a number of smaller Rigid-hulled and Rigid-Inflatable craft for various assault, patrol and security duties. There are 5.2, 6.5 and 8 metre long versions. Rigid Raiders feature GRP (glass reinforced plastic) hulls and early variants featured single or twin outboard motors. The latest RRC, the Mk3, is powered by an inboard diesel engine. They can carry up to eight troops.

SPECIALIST CRAFT

In addition to the familiar Rigid Raiding Craft and Rigid Inflatable Boats other special-ist vessels are available including air transportable Fast Insertion Craft (FIC) with a speed of 55 knots in addition to advanced wave piercing designs. Swimmer Delivery Vehicles (SDV), in reality miniature submarines, which can be deployed from dry deck shelters on larger submarines, are also operated as a part of the UK Special Forces inventory.

Since 2011 the Royal Marines have operated four CB90 Assault Craft, on loan from the Swedish Armed Forces. The aim of the trials is to gain insight into the aspects that CB90 could offer to fulfil the Royal Marines concept for a future force protection craft-which can be davit-launched from the side of a ship to protect larger ships of a Task Group from enemy fast inshore attack craft. Such vessels could also be used as a replacement for the personnel carrying landing craft.

• DANIEL FERRO   **Swimmer Delivery Vehicle**

SHIPS FOR THE FUTURE FLEET

QUEEN ELIZABETH CLASS AIRCRAFT CARRIERS

After a decade of design studies, a contract for the construction of two aircraft carriers, QUEEN ELIZABETH and PRINCE OF WALES, the largest warships to be designed and built in the UK, was signed in July 2008 between the Government and the Aircraft Carrier Alliance, an industrial group comprising BAE Systems Surface Ships, Babcock Marine, Thales and the Ministry of Defence.

The ships are being built in sections constructed by BAE Systems at Govan, Scotstoun and Portsmouth; Babcock in Rosyth and Appledore; Cammell Laird in Birkenhead and A & P, Tyne and are being assembled in Number 1 Dock at Rosyth. The dock at Rosyth has had the entrance widened from 124 feet to 138 feet. The sides were re-profiled with the removal of angled steps to make the dock floor 30 feet wider. A new overhead crane with a span of 394 feet, named Goliath, has been installed to straddle the dock and lift the smaller blocks into place. The individual blocks are built under cover and fitted out with machinery and sub-assemblies such as diesel generators, offices, cabins and galleys before they are moved to Rosyth.

The completed ships will be 284 metres long with a waterline beam of 39 metres and beam across the flight deck of 73 metres. Height from the bottom of the hull to the masthead will be 57.5 metres and draught 11 metres. There are 9 decks in the hull with another 9 in the two islands. Each ship is expected to be in the dock for two years and will be 'floated out' into the adjacent non-tidal basin for completion. The 2010 SDSR determined that the new carriers should operate the conventional F-35C 'tail-hook' variant of the Joint Strike fighter, rather than the intended F-35B VSTOL variant and be converted for 'cat & trap' operations. The Conversion Development Phase was scheduled to run to late 2012. However, concerns as to the affordability of the CV conversion prompted the MoD to reconsider the STOVL option in an attempt to finalise its PR12 budget planning round and balance the equipment programme.

According to the MoD, work undertaken had revealed that the CV-capable carrier strike capability would not be ready until 2023, some three years later than originally planned. Furthermore, the cost of fitting the Electromagnetic Aircraft Launch System (EMALS), Advanced Arresting Gear (AAG) and other CV aviation systems into PRINCE OF WALES was now estimated at £2 billion, over double the initial estimate of £950 million.

In his statement to parliament, the Secretary of State for Defence said that the SDSR decision on carriers "was right at the time, but the facts have changed and therefore so too must our approach".

He added: "Carrier strike with 'cats and traps' using the Carrier Variant jet no longer represents the best way of delivering carrier strike and I am not prepared to tolerate a three year further delay to reintroducing our Carrier Strike capability." The MoD initially said that about £40 million had been spent to date on the carrier Conversion Development Phase. However, he later admitted that the total cost of the u-turn, taking into account other costs and penalties, came to about £100 million.

QUEEN ELIZABETH is now structurally complete with the ski-jump being fitted in November 2013 (see photograph). Her drydock is due to be flooded this year and she will be moved to an alongside jetty to continue fitting out, thereby allowing the first blocks of PRINCE OF WALES to enter the drydock for her hull assembly phase. QUEEN ELIZABETH is due to start sea trials in 2017. The MoD stated that reverting to the F-35B would enable ship/aviation integration trials to begin in 2018, allowing an initial operating capability from sea in 2020.

TYPE 26 FRIGATE (GLOBAL COMBAT SHIP)

In late 2013 BAE Systems awarded four key design contracts for the Type 26 Global Combat Ship - the RN's next generation complex warships. The Design Development Agreements with Rolls-Royce, MTU, David Brown Gear Systems and Rohde & Schwarz cover propulsion and communications equipment for the ship design.

The ships will employ a Combined Diesel Electric or Gas Turbine propulsion system. This will enable the ships to achieve high speeds, whilst also providing an economic power to the onboard systems and will allow the ships to operate quietly in cruising mode. Rolls-Royce has been selected as the design partner for Gas Turbines, while David Brown Gear Systems Ltd will develop the Gear box and MTU the Diesel Generator Sets. Rohde & Schwarz has been selected to design the Integrated Communications System for the ships.

The Assessment Phase for the Type 26 programme began in March 2010, with a joint team of 550 engineers from BAE Systems, MoD and wider industry working across Bristol, Portsmouth and Glasgow to develop the detailed specification for the ships.

The MoD is expected to make its Main Investment decision around the middle of the decade, with manufacturing planned to start in 2016 and the first Type 26 set to enter service as soon as possible after 2020. The planning assumption is for a Class of 13 anti-submarine warfare and general purpose ships to replace the Type 23 frigates.

MILITARY AFLOAT REACH AND SUSTAINABILITY (MARS)

The future re-equipment of the RFA rests with this programme in which it is envisioned 11 ships will be procured (Five fleet tankers - delivered 2011 to 2015; Three joint sea-based logistics vessels - 2016, 2017 and 2020; Two fleet solid-support ships - 2017 and 2020 and a single fleet tanker - 2021).

At the end of 2007 the MoD invited industry to express their interest in the project to build up to six fleet tankers. In May 2008 four companies had been shortlisted to submit proposals for the design and construction of the ships however, this project was deferred in December 2008, the MoD announcing that having reviewed all the components of the MARS fleet auxiliary programme it was concluded that there was scope for considering alternative approaches to its procurement. Post SDSR the government stated that the requirement for the MARS programme is driven by the logistic support needs of the future RN; these being assessed following the outcome of the SDSR. It now seems likely that MARS will deliver just seven vessels (four tankers and up to three solid-support ships).

In February 2012 the MoD announced that Daewoo Shipbuilding and Marine Engineering (DSME) of South Korea were the preferred bidder in a £425 million contract to build four 37,000 tonne tankers for the RFA, the first of which is planned to enter service in 2016. They will form a new Tide class, being named TIDESPRING, TIDERACE, TIDESURGE and TIDEFORCE. DSME are drawing up detailed plans to begin construction, at Okpo-dong, south-east Korea, in 2014 .

The principal particulars of the design include an overall length of 200.9 metres, a breadth of 28.6 metres, a draught of 10 metres, and a displacement (full load) of just over 37,000 tonnes. Replenishment facilities comprise: three abeam RAS(L) stations (two sited starboard and one to port) for diesel oil, aviation fuel and fresh water; solid RAS reception up to 2 tonnes; and vertical replenishment using an embarked helicopter (the design features a flight deck sized for a Merlin, a maintenance hangar, and an in-flight refuelling capability). Provision is also made for the future fit of a stern fuel delivery reel.

With the tanker programme now under contract, the MoD is turning its attention towards the other MARS component in the shape of the Future Solid Support (FSS) programme. This second element of the modernisation of the RFA is intended to introduce replacements for RFAs FORT AUSTIN, FORT ROSALIE and FORT VICTORIA from the early 2020s.

The FSS design will deliver bulk ammunition, dry stores and food to support both carrier strike and littoral manoeuvre operations. Current plans assume a total of three FSS vessels, each displacing approximately 40,000 tonnes.

SUCCESSOR SUBMARINE PROGRAMME

The Successor programme envisages the delivery of three or four SSBNs to replace the RN's four existing Vanguard-class submarines from 2028 to maintain continuous at-sea deterrence (CASD). Initial gate approval was announced by the MoD in May 2011, marking the transition from the programme's concept phase to the current assessment phase. Assessment phase activities will finalise the Successor design, fund long lead items and start industrialisation to support manufacture. However, the key main gate investment decision - which will commit to construction and also determine whether CASD can be delivered by three or four boats - will not be taken until 2016.

Work on the concept design phase for a submarine to replace the Vanguard class has been ongoing since 2007, but this has now completed, and an outline submarine design has been selected.

In 2012 two contracts worth £350 million each were awarded by the MoD to enable detailed design work to continue on both the submarine design and the new PWR3 nuclear reactor. Although a decision on the final design and build will not be made until 2016, detailed work has to take place now to ensure that the Successor submarines can begin to be delivered in 2028.

In 2013 the Government *Trident Alternatives Review* was published, looking at various alternatives to the CASD currently provided by Trident. Although various options were put forward, including air surface and land launched systems or cruise missiles as an alternative to ballistic missiles, the current method, with four submarines seemed to be the best way to deliver CASD.

THE ROYAL FLEET AUXILIARY

The Royal Fleet Auxiliary (RFA) is a civilian manned fleet, owned by the Ministry of Defence. Traditionally, its main task has been to replenish warships of the Royal Navy at sea with fuel, food, stores and ammunition to extend their operations away from base support. However, as the RN surface fleet has shrunk, the RFA has shrunk with it and a 'Value for Money' (VfM) review is being conducted to determine how best the support provided by the RFA can be delivered to the fleet.

Legislation banning the use of single-hulled tankers in 2010 is driving the need for replacement ships. There are three such dedicated tankers in-service with the RFA with a further general replenishment ship that has a tanking capability. However, such is the delay in the new tanker programme that the two Rover class tankers have had their service lives extended by a further seven years - making them 42 years old before they are expected to finally pay off.

As part of the Military Afloat Reach and Sustainability (MARS) programme, the MoD placed an order in 2012 for four tankers to be built in South Korea. They will be named TIDESPRING, TIDERACE, TIDESURGE and TIDEFORCE (see page 45).

The long term maintenance of the RFA fleet rests with shipyards in the North West, North East and South West of England. Cammell Laird Shiprepairers & Shipbuilders Ltd of Birkenhead and the A&P Group in Falmouth and Newcastle-upon-Tyne were named as the contractors to maintain the flotilla of 16 RFA tankers, stores and landing ships. They maintain 'clusters' of ships, providing the necessary refuelling and refit work for the RFA vessels throughout their service lives. Ships are grouped in clusters according to their duties and capabilities. A&P Group are charged with two clusters (Cluster 1: ARGUS and Cluster 2: CARDIGAN BAY, LYME BAY, MOUNTS BAY) in a contract worth around £53 million with the work to be shared between its bases in Falmouth and on the Tyne, while CL Ltd is contracted for the maintenance of four clusters of ships (Cluster 3: ORANGELEAF, BLACK ROVER, GOLD ROVER; Cluster 4: DILIGENCE, WAVE KNIGHT, WAVE RULER; Cluster 5: FORT AUSTIN, FORT ROSALIE and Cluster 6: FORT VICTORIA), with contracts totalling over £180 million. The programme is expected to save over £330 million on the previous arrangements which saw individual contracts competed for as and when they were required.

SHIPS OF THE ROYAL FLEET AUXILIARY
Pennant Numbers

Ship	Pennant Number	Page	Ship	Pennant Number	Page
Tankers			**Amphibious Ships**		
ORANGELEAF	A110	50	LYME BAY	L3007	54
GOLD ROVER	A271	51	MOUNTS BAY	L3008	54
BLACK ROVER	A273	51	CARDIGAN BAY	L3009	54
WAVE KNIGHT	A389	49			
WAVE RULER	A390	49	**Repair Ship**		
			DILIGENCE	A132	55
Stores Ships					
FORT ROSALIE	A385	52	**Primary Casualty Receiving Ship/Aviation Training Ship**		
FORT AUSTIN	A386	52			
			ARGUS	A135	56
Stores Ship/Tankers					
FORT VICTORIA	A387	53			

RFA Wave Knight

FAST FLEET TANKERS

WAVE CLASS

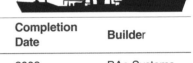

Ship	Pennant Number	Completion Date	Builder
WAVE KNIGHT	A 389	2002	BAe Systems
WAVE RULER	A 390	2002	BAe Systems

Displacement 31,500 tons (Full Load) **Dimensions** 196 x 27 x 10m **Speed** 18 knots **Armament** 2 x Vulcan Phalanx, 2 x 30mm **Aircraft** Up to 2 Merlin **Complement** 80 (plus 22 Fleet Air Arm)

Notes
These 31,500-tonne ships are diesel-electric powered, with three refueling rigs. They have a cargo capacity of 16,900 tonnes (Fuel) and 915 tonnes (Dry Stores). They have a large one spot flight deck, hangar and maintenance facilities capable of supporting two Merlin helicopters. They have spent extended periods in the Caribbean conducting successful counter-narcotics operations with an embarked RN helicopter.

RFA Orangeleaf

SUPPORT TANKERS

LEAF CLASS

Ship	Pennant Number	Completion Date	Builder
ORANGELEAF	A110	1982	Cammell Laird

Displacement 37,747 tons **Dimensions** 170m x 26m x 12m **Speed** 14.5 knots **Complement** 60

Notes

A single-hulled ex-merchant ship, originally acquired for employment mainly on freighting duties. A commercial Stat32 class tanker modified to enable it to refuel warships at sea. In 2007 she completed a Service Life Extension Programme (SLEP) refit which will enable her planned decommissioning in 2015. She underwent a further refit in 2012

The MoD also has the commercial tanker MAERSK RAPIER under charter. She is a multi-tasked tanker which supplies fuel to the naval facilities in the UK and abroad. The MoD charters the vessel to commercial companies when it is not in use for their own requirements.

RFA Black Rover

SMALL FLEET TANKERS

ROVER CLASS

Ship	Pennant Number	Completion Date	Builder
GOLD ROVER	A271	1974	Swan Hunter
BLACK ROVER	A273	1974	Swan Hunter

Displacement 11,522 tons **Dimensions** 141m x 19m x 7m **Speed** 18 knots **Armament** 2 - 20mm guns **Complement** 49/54

Notes

Small Fleet Tankers designed to supply warships with fresh water, dry cargo and refrigerated provisions, as well as a range of fuels and lubricants. Helicopter deck, but no hangar. Have been employed in recent years mainly as support for HM Ships operating around the Falkland Islands and as the FOST station tanker. Now 40 years old, GOLD ROVER was scheduled to decommission in 2009 and BLACK ROVER in 2010, but delays to the MARS programme have moved these dates back to 2016 and 2017 respectively.

RFA Fort Austin

STORES VESSELS
FORT CLASS I

Ship	Pennant Number	Completion Date	Builder
FORT ROSALIE	A385	1978	Scott Lithgow
FORT AUSTIN	A386	1979	Scott Lithgow

Displacement 23,384 tons **Dimensions** 183m x 24m x 9m **Armament** 2 x Vulcan Phalanx **Speed** 20 knots **Complement** 201, (120 RFA, 36 MoD Civilians & 45 Fleet Air Arm)

Notes

Full hangar and maintenance facilities are provided and up to four Sea King or Lynx helicopters can be carried for both the transfer of stores and anti-submarine protection of a group of ships (note: these ships are not cleared to operate Merlin). Both ships can be armed with 4 - 20mm guns. FORT AUSTIN began a regeneration refit in 2011 having been laid up at Portsmouth since 2009. She emerged from refit in September 2012 for trials and sea training prior to rejoining the fleet. Prior to sailing for the Cougar 13 deployment FORT AUSTIN received two Vulcan Phalanx mounts sited to port and starboard above the bridge wings (see photograph). FORT AUSTIN is scheduled to decommission in 2021 and FORT ROSALIE in 2022.

RFA Fort Victoria

REPLENISHMENT SHIPS
FORT CLASS II

Ship	Pennant Number	Completion Date	Builder
FORT VICTORIA	A387	1992	Harland & Wolff

Displacement 35,500 tons **Dimensions** 204m x 30m x 9m **Speed** 20 knots **Armament** 4 - 30mm guns, 2 x Phalanx CIWS, Sea Wolf Missile System (Fitted for but not with) **Complement** 100 (RFA), 24 MoD Civilians, 32 RN and up to 122 Fleet Air Arm

Notes

A "One stop" replenishment ship with the widest range of armaments, fuel and spares carried. Can operate up to 5 Sea King/Lynx or 3 Merlin Helicopters (more in a ferry role) with full maintenance facilities onboard. Medical facilities were upgraded with a 12 bed surgical capability.   Under current plans she is to remain in service until 2019. In September 2013 she took over as flagship of Combined Task Force 151 tackling piracy off Somalia.

RFA Lyme Bay

LANDING SHIP DOCK (AUXILIARY) BAY CLASS

Ship	Pennant Number	Completion Date	Builder
LYME BAY	L3007	2007	Swan Hunter
MOUNTS BAY	L3008	2006	BAe Systems
CARDIGAN BAY	L3009	2007	BAe Systems

Displacement 16,190 tonnes **Dimensions** 176.6m x 26.4m x 5.1m **Speed** 18 knots **Armament** 2 x Vulcan Phalanx in some **Complement** 60

Notes

The dock is capable of operating LCU 10s and they carry two LCVP Mk5s. They can offload at sea, over the horizon. In addition to their war fighting role they could be well suited to disaster relief and other humanitarian missions. Since 2010, vessels emerging from refit have received two funnels running up the side of the midships gantry. These were resited due to problems with fumes over the aft end of the flightdeck. Additional mini-gun emplacements have been added at the stern (in place of the aft funnels) and amidships. CARDIGAN BAY is deployed to the Gulf and is fitted with two Phalanx CIWS mounts to port and starboard. LYME BAY emerged from refit with Phalanx mounts sited forward of the superstructure and on top of the aft end of the superstructure. On 16 October she joined Operation Atalanta, as part of the EU's counter piracy Naval Force off Somalia.

RFA Diligence

FORWARD REPAIR SHIP

Ship	Pennant Number	Completion Date	Builder
DILIGENCE	A132	1981	Oesundsvarvet

Displacement 10,595 tons **Dimensions** 120m x 12m x 3m **Speed** 15 knots **Armament** 2 - 20mm **Complement** RFA 40, RN Personnel - approx 100

Notes

Formerly the M/V STENA INSPECTOR purchased (£25m) for service in the South Atlantic. Her deep diving complex was removed. She is fitted with a wide range of workshops for hull and machinery repairs, as well as facilities for supplying electricity, water, fuel, air, steam, cranes and stores to other ships and submarines. When not employed on battle repair duties she can serve as a support vessel for MCMVs and submarines on deployment. She underwent a refit in 2012 and returned to service in 2013. She successfully conducted trials on the Clyde with AMBUSH to test her ability to support the Astute class submarines away from port. Deployed as part of the Response Force Task Group in 2013 she remained deployed east of Suez in support of National Tasking.

RFA Argus

PRIMARY CASUALTY RECEIVING
SHIP/AVIATION TRAINING SHIP

Ship	Pennant Number	Completion Date	Builder
ARGUS	A135	1981	Cantieri Navali Breda

Displacement 28,481 tons (full load) **Dimensions** 175m x 30m x 8m **Speed** 18 knots
Armament 4 - 30 mm, 2 - 20 mm **Complement** 254 (inc 137 Fleet Air Arm)
Aircraft 6 Sea King/Merlin.

Notes

The former M/V CONTENDER BEZANT was purchased in 1984 and rebuilt at Harland
and Wolff, Belfast, from 1984-87 to operate as an Aviation Training Ship. She undertook a
rapid conversion in October 1990 to become a Primary Casualty Receiving Ship (PCRS)
for service in the Gulf. These facilities were upgraded and made permanent during 2001.
In 2009 the ship underwent a Service Life Extension Programme at Falmouth to switch her
primary role to that of PCRS with a secondary aviation training role. The conversion has
reduced helicopter capability by one landing spot and increased the efficiency of the primary care facility. Work undertaken included the construction of new casualty access lifts
together with a new deckhouse aft of the superstructure; upgrade and structural modification to the bridge front; accommodation upgrades to cabins, galley & crew area; removal
of starboard side vehicle ramp and installation of four additional watertight bulkheads. She
has facilities for undertaking 3 major operations simultaneously, intensive care, high
dependency and general wards for up to 100 patients. It also has a dentistry operating the-
atre, CT scanner and X-ray units. The care facility operates with a staff of up to 250 doc-
tors, nurses and support staff. The ship is scheduled to remain in service until 2020.

MV Anvil Point

STRATEGIC SEALIFT RO-RO VESSELS
POINT CLASS

Ship	Pennant Number	Completion Date	Builder
HURST POINT		2002	Flensburger
HARTLAND POINT		2002	Harland & Wolff
EDDYSTONE		2002	Flensburger
ANVIL POINT		2003	Harland & Wolff

Displacement 10,000 tonnes, 13,300 tonnes (FL) **Dimensions** 193m x 26m x 6.6m
Speed 18 knots **Complement** 38

Notes

Foreland Shipping Limited operated 6 ro-ro vessels built at yards in the UK and Germany under a PFI deal which was signed with the MoD on 27 June 2002 and runs until 31 December 2024. While the current main focus is on transporting equipment to and from the Middle East/Gulf in support of military activities in Afghanistan, the vessels also make regular voyages to the Falkland Islands and to Canada and Norway in support of training exercises. The ships are all named after English lighthouses. The ships come under the operational umbrella of Defence Supply Chain Operation and Movements (DSCOM), part of the Defence Logistics Organisation. Following a review of the MoDs strategic sealift requirement in autumn 2011, it concluded that better value for money would be achieved if the number of vessels contracted as part of this PFI was reduced from six to four. This reduction became effective on 27 April 2012, but was not made public until 2013. BEACHY HEAD and LONGSTONE, which historically operated on commercial charter, are the ships released from the Strategic Ro-Ro PFI and will be sold to external commercial interests in 2014.

HMS LANCASTER

Crown Copyright/MoD 2013

HMS BULWARK

Crown Copyright/MoD 2013

HMS DRAGON

HMS PROTECTOR

Leo Marriott

RFA FORT VICTORIA replenishes RFA FORT AUSTIN to starboard and HMS ILLUSTRIOUS to port)

Crown Copyright/MoD 2013

David Hannaford

SD BOVISAND approaching three TUTT class tugs at Devonport

SERCO MARINE SERVICES

In December 2007 the MoD signed a £1 billion Private Finance Initiative (PFI) contract with Serco Denholm Marine Services Limited for the future provision of marine services (FPMS) over the following 15 years. In 2009 Serco bought out Denholm's share and the SD funnel logos have been replaced by a prominent Serco logo on the superstructure.

Marine services embrace a wide range of waterborne and associated support activities, both in and out of port, at Portsmouth, Devonport and on the Clyde, as well as maintenance of UK and overseas moorings and navigational marks and support of a range of military operations and training.

In-port services include the provision of berthing and towage activities within the three naval bases; passenger transportation, including pilot transfers and the transportation of stores, including liquids and munitions. The recovery and disposal of waste from ships and spillage prevention and clean-up also fall within their tasking. There is also a requirement for substantial out-of-port operations. Diving training, minelaying exercises, torpedo recovery, boarding training and target towing duties are also undertaken.

The Briggs Group has been sub-contracted to assist with buoys and mooring support work. Shore based work to support these moorings and navigation buoys, have been relocated from Pembroke Dock to Burntisland on the Firth of Forth.

Initially all vessels were repainted with red funnels and black hulls, the white line having been removed as were, in most cases, the pennant numbers. All names are now prefixed with the letters 'SD' and all vessels fly the red ensign. In 2012, the last vestiges of the former RMAS identity were removed as, gradually, the whole fleet is to adopt a new colour scheme with the buff superstructure being repainted white.

SHIPS OF
SERCO MARINE SERVICES

Ship	Page	Ship	Page
SD ADEPT	69	SD MOORFOWL	87
SD BOUNTIFUL	68	SD MOORHEN	87
SD BOVISAND	78	SD NAVIGATOR	88
SD CAREFUL	69	SD NETLEY	79
SD CATHERINE	73	SD NEWHAVEN	79
SD CAWSAND	78	SD NORTHERN RIVER	86
SD CHRISTINA	71	SD NORTON	82
SD CLYDE RACER	89	SD NUTBOURNE	79
SD CLYDE SPIRIT	90	SD OBAN	81
SD DEBORAH	71	SD OCEANSPRAY	85
SD DEPENDABLE	68	SD OILMAN	85
SD EILEEN	71	SD OMAGH	81
SD EMILY	73	SD ORONSAY	81
SD ENGINEER	83	SD PADSTOW	80
SD EVA	83	SD POWERFUL	69
SD FAITHFUL	69	SD RAASAY	88
SD FLORENCE	72	SD RELIABLE	68
SD FORCEFUL	69	SD RESOURCEFUL	68
SD FRANCES	72	SD SOLENT RACER	89
SD GENEVIEVE	72	SD SOLENT SPIRIT	90
SD HELEN	72	SD SUZANNE	71
SD HERCULES	70	SD TAMAR RACER	89
SD IMPETUS	66	SD TAMAR SPIRIT	90
SD IMPULSE	66	SD TEESDALE	85
SD INDEPENDENT	67	SD TILLY	74
SD INDULGENT	67	SD VICTORIA	75
SD INSPECTOR	83	SD WARDEN	76
SD JUPITER	70	SD WATERPRESS	85
SD KYLE OF LOCHALSH	77		
SD MARS	70	**BRIGGS SUB-CONTRACT**	
SD MELTON	84		
SD MENAI	84	CAMERON	91
SD MEON	84	KINGDOM OF FIFE	91

SD Impetus

TUGS

IMPULSE CLASS

Ship	Completion Date	Builder
SD IMPULSE	1993	R. Dunston
SD IMPETUS	1993	R. Dunston

G.R.T. 400 tons approx **Dimensions** 33m x 10m x 4m **Speed** 12 knots **Complement** 5

Notes

Completed in 1993 specifically to serve as berthing tugs for the Trident Class submarines at Faslane. To be retained in service until 2022.

SD Independent

ASD 2509 CLASS

Ship	Completion Date	Builder
SD INDEPENDENT	2009	Damen, Gorinchem
SD INDULGENT	2009	Damen, Gorinchem

G.R.T. 345 tons approx **Dimensions** 26.09m x 9.44m x 4.3m **Speed** 13 knots **Complement** 5

Notes

Azimuth Stern Drive (ASD) tugs. Designed for Coastal and Harbour towage, specifically modified for making cold moves within the Naval Bases. Both are based at Portsmouth.

SD Bountiful

ATD 2909 CLASS

Ship	Completion Date	Builder
SD RELIABLE	2009	Damen, Stellendam
SD BOUNTIFUL	2010	Damen, Stellendam
SD RESOURCEFUL	2010	Damen, Stellendam
SD DEPENDABLE	2010	Damen, Stellendam

G.R.T. 271 tons **Dimensions** 29.14m x 9.98m x 4.8m **Speed** 13.1 knots **Complement** 5 (Accommodation for 6)

Notes

Azimuthing Tractor Drive (ATD) tugs. SD BOUNTIFUL is based at Portsmouth. SD RESOURCEFUL, SD RELIABLE and SD DEPENDABLE are based on the Clyde. Designed for Coastal and Harbour towage, specifically modified for making cold moves within the Naval Bases. Two double drum towing winches are fitted, along with extensive underwater fendering, fire fighting equipment and facilities for passenger and stores transportation.

SD Powerful

TWIN UNIT TRACTOR TUGS

Ship	Completion Date	Builder
SD ADEPT	1980	R. Dunston
SD CAREFUL	1982	R. Dunston
SD FAITHFUL	1985	R. Dunston
SD FORCEFUL	1985	R. Dunston
SD POWERFUL	1985	R. Dunston

G.R.T. 384 tons **Dimensions** 38.8m x 9.42m x 4m **Speed** 12 knots **Complement** 5

Notes

The principal harbour tugs in naval service. Some are to undergo a service life extension programme. SD POWERFUL returned to Portsmouth following a short transfer to Devonport to back fill any refit downtime for existing vessels.

SD Jupiter

STAN TUG 2608 CLASS

Ship	Completion Date	Builder
SD HERCULES	2009	Damen, Gorinchem
SD JUPITER	2009	Damen, Gorinchem
SD MARS	2009	Damen, Gorinchem

G.R.T. 133.92 tons **Dimensions** 26.61m x 8.44m x 4.05m **Speed** 12 knots **Complement** 4 (6 max)

Notes

A conventional Twin Screw Tug design. SD HERCULES and SD MARS are based at Devonport. SD JUPITER is based on the Clyde. All can be used to handle submarine mounted Towed Arrays.

SD Eileen

ASD 2009 CLASS

Ship	Completion Date	Builder
SD CHRISTINA	2010	Damen, Gdynia
SD DEBORAH	2010	Damen, Gdynia
SD EILEEN	2010	Damen, Gdynia
SD SUZANNE	2010	Damen, Gdynia

G.R.T. 120.74 tons **Dimensions** 21.2m x 9.4m x 3.6m **Speed** 11 knots **Complement** 3/4

Notes

Azimuth Stern Drive tugs derived from the successful Damen ASD 2411 shiphandling tug. Winches fore and aft, together with a bow thruster, make these tugs suitable for handling smaller surface ship, barge work and assisting with submarine movements. SD DEBORAH and SD EILEEN are based at Devonport, SD CHRISTINA and SD SUZANNE at Portsmouth.

SD Genevieve

FELICITY CLASS

Ship	Completion Date	Builder
SD FLORENCE	1980	R. Dunston
SD FRANCES	1980	R. Dunston
SD GENEVIEVE	1980	R. Dunston
SD HELEN	1974	R. Dunston

G.R.T. 88.96 tons **Dimensions** 22.0m x 6.4m x 2.6m **Speed** 10 knots **Complement** 4

Notes

Water Tractors used for the movement of small barges and equipment. SD FRANCES and SD FLORENCE based at Devonport, with the other pair at Portsmouth.

SD Catherine

PUSHY CAT 1204

Ship	Completion Date	Builder
SD CATHERINE	2008	Damen, Gorinchem
SD EMILY	2008	Damen, Gorinchem

G.R.T. 29.4 tons **Dimensions** 12.3m x 4.13m x 1.55m **Speed** 8 knots **Complement** 2

Notes

Powered by a single Caterpillar 3056 TA diesel driving a single screw. A propulsion nozzle is fitted, and twin rudders to give a 2.1 tons bollard pull. SD CATHERINE is based at Portsmouth, SD EMILY at Devonport. General line runner and harbour workboat.

SD Tilly

STAN TUG 1405

Ship	Completion Date	Builder
SD TILLY	2009	Damen, Gorinchem

G.R.T. 45 tons **Dimensions** 14.55m x 4.98m x 1.8m **Speed** 9 knots **Complement** 3

Notes

A general purpose inshore and harbour tug based at Devonport. A twin screw version of the Pushy Cat 1204. Slightly larger with a bow thruster and also developing 8 tonnes bollard pull. Line handler, general workboat and ideal for moving small barges.

SD Victoria

WORLDWIDE SUPPORT VESSEL

Ship	Completion Date	Builder
SD VICTORIA	2010	Damen, Galatz

G.R.T. 3,522 tons **Dimensions** 83m x 16m x 4.5m **Speed** 14 knots **Complement** 16 (Accommodation for 72)

Notes

Powered by two Caterpillar 3516B diesels driving two shafts with controllable pitch propellers SD VICTORIA is designed to support training operations around the world. Capable of transporting both personnel and equipment and supporting diving operations. She is equipped with classrooms, briefing rooms and operations rooms in addition to workshop facilities. There is provision to carry and operate RIBs and there is a helicopter winching deck. Note Fast Interceptor Craft under covers on the quarterdeck.

SD Warden

TRIALS VESSEL

Ship	Completion Date	Builder
SD WARDEN	1989	Richards

Displacement 626 tons **Dimensions** 48m x 10m x 4m **Speed** 15 knots **Complement** 11

Notes

Built as a Range Maintenance Vessel but now based at Kyle of Lochalsh and operated in support of BUTEC. Also operates as a Remotely Operated Vehicle (ROV) platform. A replacement ROV has been installed and set to work to replace the older system. To remain in service until 2022.

• ALISTAIR MacDONALD

SD Kyle of Lochalsh

TRIALS VESSEL

Ship	Completion Date	Builder
SD KYLE OF LOCHALSH	1997	Abel, Bristol

Displacement 120 tons **Dimensions** 24.35m x 9m x 3.45m **Speed** 10.5 knots **Complement** 4

Notes

The former twin screw tug MCS LENIE which has now been purchased from Maritime Craft Services (Clyde) Ltd by Serco Marine Services. The 24.35m tug, built in 1997 by Abel in Bristol, is powered by Caterpillar main engines producing a total of 2,200bhp for a bollard pull of 26 tons. She is used to support trials and operations at Kyle.

SD Cawsand

TENDERS
STORM CLASS

Ship	Completion Date	Builder
SD BOVISAND	1997	FBM (Cowes)
SD CAWSAND	1997	FBM (Cowes)

G.R.T 225 tonnes **Dimensions** 23m x 11m x 2m **Speed** 15 knots **Complement** 5

Notes

These craft are used in support of Flag Officer Sea Training (FOST) at Plymouth to transfer staff quickly and comfortably to and from Warships and Auxiliaries within and beyond the Plymouth breakwater in open sea conditions. These are the first vessels of a small waterplane area twin hull (SWATH) design to be ordered by the Ministry of Defence and cost £6.5 million each. Speed restrictions implemented due to wash problems generated by these vessels. To remain in service until 2022.

• DAVID WALTER   **SD Netley**

NEWHAVEN CLASS

Ship	Completion Date	Builder
SD NEWHAVEN	2000	Aluminium SB
SD NUTBOURNE	2000	Aluminium SB
SD NETLEY	2001	Aluminium SB

Tonnage 77 tonnes (45 grt) **Dimensions** 18.3m x 6.8m x 1.88m **Speed** 10 knots **Complement** 2/3 Crew (60 passengers)

Notes

MCA Class IV Passenger Vessels acquired as replacements for Fleet tenders. Employed on general passenger duties within the port area. To remain in service until 2022. SD NETLEY and NUTBOURNE are based at Portsmouth, SD NEWHAVEN at Devonport.

SD Padstow

PADSTOW CLASS

Ship	Completion Date	Builder
SD PADSTOW	2000	Aluminium SB

Tonnage 77 tonnes (45 grt) **Dimensions** 18.3m x 6.8m x 1.88m **Speed** 10 knots
Complement 2/3 Crew (60 passengers)

Notes

MCA Class IV, VI and VIA Passenger Vessel based at Devonport. Used on liberty runs
in Plymouth Sound and the Harbour as well as occasionally supporting FOST. To remain
in service until 2022.

SD Omagh

OBAN CLASS

Ship	Completion Date	Builder
SD OBAN	2000	McTay Marine
SD ORONSAY	2000	McTay Marine
SD OMAGH	2000	McTay Marine

G.R.T 199 tons **Dimensions** 27.7m x 7.30m x 3.75m **Speed** 10 knots **Complement** 4 Crew (60 passengers)

Notes

MCA Class IIA Passenger Vessels which replaced Fleet tenders in 2001. SD OBAN was transferred to Devonport in 2003 and is now primarily used to support FOST staff. SD ORONSAY and SD OMAGH employed on general passenger duties on the Clyde and are additionally classified as Cargo Ship VIII(A). To remain in service until 2022.

SD Norton

PERSONNEL FERRY

Ship	Completion Date	Builder
SD NORTON	1989	FBM Marine

G.R.T 21 tons **Dimensions** 15.8m x 5.5m x 1.5m **Speed** 13 knots **Complement** 2

Notes

The single FBM catamaran, 8837, operated at Portsmouth. Can carry 30 passengers or 2 tons of stores. Was a prototype catamaran designed to replace older Harbour Launches but no more were ordered.

SD Eva

PERSONNEL FERRY

Ship	Completion Date	Builder
SD EVA	2009	Damen

G.R.T 168 tons **Dimensions** 33.21m x 7.4m x 3.3m **Speed** 23.4 knots **Complement** 4-6 (plus 34 passengers)

Notes

Operated on the Clyde as a Fast Crew Transport. The Axe Bow design allows the vessel to effectively cut through waves with minimal movement of the vessel. The vessel is the first of its type in the UK to be operated under the International Code of Safety for High Speed Craft (HSC Code).

SD Menai

FLEET TENDERS

Ship	Completion Date	Builder
SD MELTON	1981	Richard Dunston
SD MENAI	1981	Richard Dunston
SD MEON	1982	Richard Dunston

G.R.T. 117.3 tons **Dimensions** 24m x 6.7m x 3.05m **Speed** 10.5 knots **Complement** 4 (12 passengers)

Notes

The last three survivors of a once numerous class of vessels used as Training Tenders, Passenger Ferries, or Cargo Vessels. MENAI and MEON are operated at Falmouth. MELTON is operated at Kyle. A vessel replacement programme now seems unlikely and this elderly trio are expected to remain in service until 2022.

SD Teesdale

COASTAL OILER

Ship	Completion Date	Builder
SD TEESDALE	1976	Yorkshire Drydock Co.

G.R.T. 499 tons **Dimensions** 43.86m x 9.5m x 3.92m **Speed** 8 knots **Complement** 5

Notes

Formerly the oil products tanker TEESDALE H operated by John H Whitaker. Operates as a parcel tanker delivering diesel and aviation fuel and also delivering / receiving compensating water. She is self propelled by two Aquamaster thrusters.

A Diesel Lighter Barge, SD OILMAN, and a Water Lighter Barge, SD WATERPRESS, are operated on the Clyde. A further barge, a Liquid Mixed Lighter Barge, SD OCEANSPRAY, is based at Portsmouth.

SD Northern River

MULTI-PURPOSE VESSEL

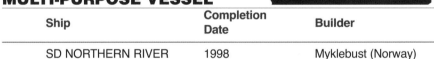

Ship	Completion Date	Builder
SD NORTHERN RIVER	1998	Myklebust (Norway)

G.R.T 3,605 tons **Dimensions** 92.8m x 18.8m x 4.9m **Speed** 14 knots **Complement** 14

Notes

Bought from Deep Ocean AS (a subsidiary of Trico Marine) this Ulstein UT-745L designed Support Vessel entered service with Serco in March 2012. She can be employed on a variety of tasking from target towing, through noise ranging to data gathering; boarding training to submarine escort. Her extensive flat work deck allows her to embark containers for passive sonar training. She can also provide nuclear emergency support as well as support to submarine emergencies. She can deploy with the NATO Submarine Rescue System embarked (see photo). She can also support the Submarine Parachute Assistance Group.

SD Moorhen

DIVING SUPPORT VESSELS
MOOR CLASS

Ship	Completion Date	Builder
SD MOORFOWL	1989	McTay Marine
SD MOORHEN	1989	McTay Marine

Displacement 518 tons **Dimensions** 32m x 11m x 2m **Speed** 8 knots **Complement** 10

Notes

Designed as a powered mooring lighter for use within sheltered coastal waters the lifting horns have been removed from the bows of both vessels when they were converted to Diving Support Vessels. They are used by the Defence Diving School for diving training in the Kyle of Lochalsh. To remain in service until 2022.

SD Raasay

MULTICAT 2510 CLASS

Ship	Completion Date	Builder
SD NAVIGATOR	2009	Damen, Hardinxveld
SD RAASAY	2010	Damen, Hardinxveld

G.R.T 150.27 tons **Dimensions** 26.3m x 10.64m x 2.55m **Speed** 8 knots **Complement** 3 (plus up to 12 additional personnel)

Notes

SD NAVIGATOR is equipped for buoy handling with a single 9 ton capacity crane. She is capable of supporting diving operations. SD RAASAY is based at the Kyle of Lochalsh. She is fitted with two cranes for torpedo recovery and support diving training. SD NAVIGATOR is managed from Portsmouth, but operates between Devonport and Portsmouth. Two similar vessels, SD INSPECTOR (ex-DMS EAGLE) and SD ENGINEER operate from Portsmouth and Devonport respectively.

SD Solent Racer

STAN TENDER 1505 CLASS

Ship	Completion Date	Builder
SD CLYDE RACER	2008	Damen, Gorinchem
SD SOLENT RACER	2008	Damen, Gorinchem
SD TAMAR RACER	2008	Damen, Gorinchem

Displacement 25.19 GRT **Dimensions** 16m x 4.85m x 1.25m **Speed** 20 knots **Complement** 3 (+ 10 Passengers)

Notes

Of aluminium construction these boats are employed on transfer of pilots, port security operations and passenger and VIP transportation.

SD Solent Spirit

STAN TENDER 1905 CLASS

Ship	Completion Date	Builder
SD CLYDE SPIRIT	2008	Damen, Gorinchem
SD SOLENT SPIRIT	2008	Damen, Gorinchem
SD TAMAR SPIRIT	2008	Damen, Gorinchem

Displacement 43.3 GRT **Dimensions** 18.91m x 5.06m x 1.65m **Speed** 21.7 knots **Complement** 3 (+ 10 passengers)

Notes

Steel hull with aluminium superstructure. Special propeller tunnels are fitted to increase propulsion efficiency and to reduce vibration and noise levels. These vessels are able to operate safely and keep good performance in wind speeds up to Force 6 and wave heights of 2 metres. Employed on transfer of pilots, VIPs and personnel.

Kingdom of Fife

ANCHOR HANDLING TUG

Ship	Completion Date	Builder
KINGDOM OF FIFE	2008	Damen, Galatz

Displacement 1,459 tons **Dimensions** 61.2m x 13.5m x 4.75m **Speed** 13.7 knots
Complement 18

Notes

Briggs Marine won a £100m contract from Serco to support navigation buoy maintenance and mooring support for the Royal Navy for 15 years. During the contract period, Briggs Marine provide support for over 350 moorings, navigation buoys and targets
for the RN all around the UK coast, as well as Cyprus, Gibraltar and the Falkland
Islands. KINGDOM OF FIFE was delivered in May 2008 and supports the existing
Briggs Marine shallow draught and heavy lift craft CAMERON in servicing the contract,
and is equipped with a decompression chamber and its own dedicated dive support
team.

Smit Dart

AIRCREW TRAINING VESSELS

Ship	Comp Date	Builder	Base Port
SMIT DEE	2003	BES Rosyth	Buckie
SMIT DART	2003	BES Rosyth	Plymouth
SMIT DON	2003	BES Rosyth	Blyth
SMIT YARE	2003	FBMA Cebu	Great Yarmouth
SMIT TOWY	2003	FBMA Cebu	Pembroke Dock
SMIT SPEY	2003	FBMA Cebu	Plymouth

G.R.T. 95.86 GRT **Dimensions** 27.6m x 6.6m x 1.5m **Speed** 21 knots **Complement** 6

Notes

The service for Marine Support to Ranges and Aircrew Training is provided by SMIT (Scotland) Ltd and runs until April 2017. These vessels provide training for military aircrew in marine survival techniques, helicopter winching drills, target towing and general marine support tasks. More recently they have participated in Navy Command boarding exercises, simulating arms and drug smuggling activities and force protection exercises involving both Fast Attack Craft and Fast Inshore Attack Craft. SMIT DART completed as a passenger vessel with a larger superstructure. A smaller, second-hand vessel, SMIT TAMAR is employed in a similar role.

Smit Wey

RANGE SAFETY VESSELS

Ship	Comp Date	Builder
SMIT STOUR	2003	Maritime Partners Norway
SMIT ROTHER	2003	Maritime Partners Norway
SMIT ROMNEY	2003	Maritime Partners Norway
SMIT CERNE	2003	Maritime Partners Norway
SMIT FROME	2003	Maritime Partners Norway
SMIT MERRION	2003	Maritime Partners Norway
SMIT PENALLY	2003	Maritime Partners Norway
SMIT WEY	2003	Maritime Partners Norway
SMIT NEYLAND	2003	Maritime Partners Norway

G.R.T. 7.0 tons **Dimensions** 12.3m x 2.83m x 0.89m **Speed** 35 knots **Complement** 2

Notes

A class of 12 metre Fast Patrol Craft which operate on Range Safety Duties at Dover, Portland and Pembroke.

• DEREK FOX

RCTV Arezzo

ARMY VESSELS
RAMPED CRAFT LOGISTIC

Vessel	Pennant Number	Completion Date	Builder
ARROMANCHES	L105	1987	James & Stone
ANDALSNES	L107	1984	James & Stone
AACHEN	L110	1986	James & Stone
AREZZO	L111	1986	James & Stone
AUDEMER	L113	1987	James & Stone

Displacement 290 tonnes (Laden) **Dimensions** 33.3m x 8.3m x 1.5m **Speed** 10 knots
Complement 6.

Notes

Operated by the Army's 17 Port and Maritime Regiment, Royal Logistic Corps, these all purpose landing craft are capable of carrying up to 96 tons. They are self sustaining for around five days or a thousand nautical miles before requiring replenishment either at sea or in a haven. In service in UK coastal waters. ANDALSNES is operated by 417 Maritime Troop at Cyprus. ARROMANCHES was formerly AGHEILA (re-named 1994 when original vessel was sold). Most vessels sport a green and black camouflage scheme.

94

AWB Storm

WORK BOATS

Vessel	Pennant Number	Completion Date	Builder
STORM	WB41	2008	Warbreck Eng.
DIABLO	WB42	2008	Warbreck Eng.
MISTRAL	WB43	2008	Warbreck Eng.
SIROCCO	WB44	2008	Warbreck Eng.

Displacement 48 tonnes **Dimensions** 14.75m x 4.30m x 0.0m **Speed** 10 knots
Complement 4

Notes

Part of the Army's strategic port operations in Southampton, but can be transported by a 'mother ship' to other ports and places like Iraq. Are often used as tugs for mexeflotes, positioning other pontoon equipment and for handling flexible pipelines. They have a fire-fighting capability.

The Army also operate a number of smaller Combat Support Boats. Built by RTK Marine/VT Halmatic (now BAE) these are fast and rugged small craft, 8.8m long with a twin Hamilton waterjet propulsion system powered by twin 210hp diesel engines.

BORDER FORCE
STAN PATROL 4207 CLASS

Vessel	Pennant Number	Completion Date	Builder
SEARCHER	-	2002	Damen
SEEKER	-	2001	Damen
VALIANT	-	2004	Damen
VIGILANT	-	2003	Damen

Displacement 238 GRT   **Dimensions** 42.8m x 7.11m x 2.52m   **Speed** 26+ knots
Complement 12

Notes
Powered by two Caterpillar diesel engines these vessels are capable of reaching speeds above 26 knots. They are able to remain at sea for extended periods and in heavy weather conditions. They operate 24 hours a day, 365 days per year, through the employment of dual crews. There are ten crews for the five Border Force cutters comprising 120 seagoing staff, working two weeks on and two weeks off. Cutters are mostly deployed on a risk-led or intelligence-led basis detecting prohibited and restricted goods, boarding and searching ships and providing a law enforcement presence in remote and inaccesible areas. Vessels are prefixed HMC for Her Majesty's Cutter. The are recognised by a diagonal Blue,white, red, white stripe on the bows.

TELKKÄ CLASS

Vessel	Pennant Number	Completion Date	Builder
PROTECTOR	-	2002	UKI Workboat

Displacement 400 tonnes   **Dimensions** 49.7m x 7.5m x 3.9m   **Speed** 22 knots
Complement 12

Notes

In 2013 the Border Force purchased the former Finnish Border Agency vessel TAVI. Built by Uki Workboat Ltd, Uusikaupunki, Finland she is powered by 2 x Wärtsilä 12V200 Diesel Engines. She has replaced SENTINEL which was withdrawn from service in June 2013.

Babcock was awarded a contract by the Border Force in June 2011, to provide through-life maintenance and support for the force's fleet of five patrol boats. Under the contract each ship undergoes a docking period every two years and annual Life Saving Appliances (LSA) periods, taking one week, alongside. All five cutters are now based at Portsmouth.

AIRCRAFT OF THE FLEET AIR ARM

LOCKHEED MARTIN

Lockheed Martin LIGHTNING FRS1

Role Strike, fighter and reconnaissance aircraft
Engine 1 x Pratt & Whitney F-135 turbofan rated at 43,000lb thrust with reheat
Length 51' 4" **Wingspan** 35' **Height** 15'
Max Weight 60,000 lbs
Max Speed Mach 1.6
Crew 1 pilot
Avionics AN/APG-81 electronically scanned radar; electro-optical targeting system; distributed aperture vision system; AN/ASQ-239 'Barracuda' electronic warfare system; helmet-mounted display system; multi-function advanced data link.
Armament 2 internal weapons bays, each with separate hard points for a 1,000lb bomb equivalent and a single AIM-120 AMRAAM are used in stealthy mode. When stealth is not required, 7 external pylons can be fitted, 3 under each wing and one under the fuselage allowing up to 12,000lb of fuel and weapons to be carried. The inner wing pylons can each carry a 426 US gallon drop tank. Software to support British weapons has not been developed and the UK MOD is procuring an initial outfit of US weapons to support the aircraft in service. The full range of US air-to-air and air-to-ground weapons can be carried.
Squadron Service 809 Naval Air squadron to be formed.

Notes
Strike operations using stealth to defeat sophisticated air defence systems are the Lightning's defining role but it is also a fighter and reconnaissance aircraft, hence its FRS designation. 4 British aircraft supported by RN and RAF personnel train alongside their USMC counterparts at Eglin Air Force Base in Florida. 809 NAS is due to embark in QUEEN ELIZABETH in 2020 after completion of first-of-class flying trials. It will be shore-based with other UK Lightning units at RAF Marham.

BAE Systems HAWK T 1

Role Fleet requirements and operational training aircraft.
Engine 1 x Rolls Royce Adour 151 rated at 5,200lb thrust.
Length 40' 9"   **Wingspan** 32' 7"   **Height** 13' 1"
Max Weight 20,000lb
Max Speed 540 knots
Crew 1 or 2 pilots
Avionics VHF radio. No combat systems.
Armament Can be fitted with 1 x 30mm Aden gun on a centreline pod. 2 underwing hard points can take AIM-9 Sidewinder missiles or up to 1,500lb of practice weapons.
Squadron Service 736 Naval Air squadron

Notes
12 Hawks support FOST with simulated strikes against ships undergoing sea training. Commissioned as 736 NAS in 2013, the unit has a growing number of RN pilots, maintaining skills until front-line fighter units are re-formed. In 2014 it will have a mixture of RN and civilian pilots with civilian contract maintenance. It is based at RNAS Culdrose.

AgustaWestland MERLIN HM1, HM2

Role Anti-submarine, Search and Strike and Maritime surveillance
Engine 3 x Rolls-Royce Turbomeca RTM322 turboshafts each developing 2,100 shp
Length 74' 10" **Width** 14' 10" **Height** 21' 10" **Main Rotor Diameter** 61'
Max Weight 32,120 lbs
Max Speed 167 kts   **Range** 625 nm
Crew 1 or 2 pilots, 1 observer and 1 sensor operator
Avionics Blue Kestrel 360 degree radar; Orange Reaper ESM; Folding Light Acoustic System for Helicopters (FLASH); AQS 903A acoustic processor; defence aids including directional infrared counter-measures (DIRCM), AN/AAR-57 missile approach warning system, chaff and flare dispensers; Wescam MX-15 electro-optical/IR camera fitted to a number of deployed aircraft.
Armament 1 x M3M 0.5" gun in cabin door; 1 x GPMG in cabin window; up to 4 Stingray torpedoes; up to 4 Mark 10 depth charges.
Squadron Service 814, 820, 824, 829 Naval Air Squadrons

Notes
A total of 30 helicopters upgraded to HM 2 standard being delivered to the RN with squadrons due to achieve operational capability during 2014. 814 and 820 NAS embark in the Response Force Task Group LPH and RFAs; 829 NAS provides single aircraft detachments to Type 23 frigates and 824 is the type's training and development unit. All are shore-based at RNAS Culdrose. In 2013 it was announced by the MOD that several 'role-change' modules are to be evaluated which would enable HM 2s, with further as yet un-costed modification, to operate in the airborne surveillance and control role.

AgustaWestland MERLIN HC3 and planned HC4

Role Commando assault, load-lifting and tactical helicopter operations
Engine 3 x Rolls-Royce Turbomeca RTM322 turboshafts each developing 2,100 shp
Length 74' 10" **Width** 14' 10" **Height** 21' 10" **Main Rotor Diameter** 61'
Max Weight 32,120 lbs
Max Speed 167 kts   **Range** 625 nm
Crew 1 or 2 pilots, 1 aircrewman
Avionics Defensive aids suite including directional IR counter-measures, AN/AAR-57 missile approach warning system, automatic chaff & flare dispensers; Wescam MX-15 electro-optical/IR camera
Armament 1 x M3M 0.5" gun in cabin door; 1 x 7.62mm GPMG in cabin window.
Squadron Service 846 NAS is to re-equip with Merlin HC3s in 2015 followed by 845 NAS with HC4s in 2017.

Notes
RN personnel continue to train on the HC3 but the type cannot be embarked until it is brought up to HC4 standard. This is to have the same 'glass' cockpit and power-folding rotor-head as the HM2 together with a new folding tail pylon above the rear loading ramp. Flotation gear, lashing points and new communications equipment will also be installed. HC3s and HC4s can both carry up to 24 marines in crash-resistant seating or a disposable load of up to 8,800lb.

AgustaWestland SEA KING

All marks of Sea King are to be withdrawn from service in 2016 after forty-seven years' service in the Royal Navy.

Engines 2 x 1600shp Rolls Royce Gnome H 1400 – 1 free power turbines.
Length 54' 9" **Height** 17' 2" **Max Weight** 21,400lb **Rotor Diameter** 62' 0"
Max Speed 125 knots (HC 4+ 145 knots).

NICK NEWNS

HAR 5

Roles Search and Rescue; utility; aircrew training.
Crew 2 pilots, 1 observer and 1 aircrewman/winchman.
Avionics Sea Searcher radar; Star Safire III EO/IR camera turret.
Armament A 7.62mm machine gun can be mounted in the doorway if required.
Squadron Service 771 Naval Air Squadron

Notes
771 NAS provides SAR coverage for the south-western UK from its base at RNAS Culdrose and a detachment of 3 aircraft in Prestwick which covers a vast area of Scotland, Northern Ireland and 200 miles out into the Atlantic. Civilian helicopters under a Government contract will take over SAR duties from 2016.

• LEE HOWARD

ASaC 7

Role Airborne Surveillance and Control of both maritime and land operations.
Crew 1 pilot and 2 observers.
Avionics Cerberus mission-system; Searchwater radar; Orange Crop ESM; Joint Tactical Information Distribution System (Link 16). AN/AAR-57 missile approach warning system; IR jammer, radar-warning receiver; auto chaff and flare dispenser.
Squadron Service 849, 854, 857 Naval Air Squadrons.

Notes

854 and 857 NAS detachments to Afghanistan are to end in 2014. 849 NAS is a training and development unit and all three squadrons are shore-based at RNAS Culdrose. The MoD announced the evaluation of a modularised Cerberus system or alternatives under Project Crows Nest in 2013 to be fitted in modified Merlin HM2s to replace the Sea King ASaC7s capability. The preferred equipment is to be confirmed in 2015 and will potentially achieve initial operational capability in 2018, leaving a major capability gap after 2016.

STEVE WRIGHT

HC 4

Role Commando assault, load-lifting and tactical helicopter operations.
Crew 1 or 2 pilots and 1 aircrewman. About 25% of pilots and all aircrewmen are Royal Marines.
Avionics AN/AAR-57 missile approach warning system; IR jammer; automatic chaff & flare dispenser
Armament 1 x M3M 0.5" gun in cargo door and 1 x 0.762mm GPMG in crew-entry door to give 360 degree sweeping fire when needed
Squadron Service 845, 846 and 848 Naval Air Squadrons.

Notes

There will be a two year gap in embarked capability between 2016 when the Sea King HC 4 is retired and 2018 when the first Merlin HC 4 squadron reaches operational maturity. Sea King commando helicopter operations will begin to run down in 2015 when 846 NAS re-equips with the Merlin HC 3. All three squadrons are shore-based at RNAS Yeovilton but are available at short notice to deploy. The Commando Helicopter Force forms part of the UK Joint helicopter Force which also includes Army and RAF helicopters.

DANIEL FERRO

AgustaWestland LYNX

Variants HMA 8
Roles Surface search and strike; anti-submarine strike; boarding party support.
Engines 2 x Rolls-Royce Gem BS 360-07-26 free power turbines each developing 900 shp.
Length 39' 1" **Height** 11' 0" **Max Weight** 9,500lb **Rotor diameter** 42' 0"
Max Speed 150 knots
Crew 1 pilot and 1 observer
Avionics : Sea Spray radar; Orange Crop ESM; Sea Owl Electro-Optical/Infrared camera (HMA 8); Second-generation Anti-jam Tactical UHF Radio for NATO (SATURN) including Successor IFF and Digital Signal processor.
Armament External pylons for up to 4 Sea Skua ASM or 2 Stingray torpedoes. 1 door mounted M3M 0.5" gun and 1 hand-held Heckler & Koch G 3 sniper rifle to provide Precision Anti-Personnel Sniping (PAPS) in support of boarding parties in case they are opposed.
Squadron Service 702 and 815 Naval Air Squadrons.

Notes

815 NAS provides operational flights to deployed warships and RFAs; DARING class destroyers can embark 2 Lynx, others usually 1. 702 NAS is the training and development unit and both are shore-based at RNAS Yeovilton. Lynx flights will be withdrawn gradually from service after the first Wildcat flight becomes operational in 2015.

STEVE WRIGHT

AgustaWestland WILDCAT

Variants AH 1, HMA 2.
Roles Surface search and strike; anti-submarine strike; boarding party support (HMA 2); reconnaissance and troop carrying (AH 1).
Engines: 2 x LHTEC CTS 800 turboshafts each rated at 1362shp
Length 50' 0" **Height** 12' 0" **Max Weight** 13,200lb **Rotor diameter** 42' 0"
Max Speed 157 knots **Crew** 1 pilot and 1 observer.
Avionics Selex-Galileo Sea Spray 7400E multi-mode Active Electronically Scanned Array, AESA, radar; Wescam MX-15 EO/IR camera. Defensive aids suite.
Armament Future air-to-surface guided weapon in both light and heavy versions; Stingray torpedoes; Mark 11 depth-charges; door mounted M3M 0.5" gun.
Squadron Service 847, 700W Naval Air Squadrons.

Notes
847 NAS, part of the Commando helicopter Force, is to become the first operational Wildcat AH 1 unit when it re-equips in 2014. 700W is an intensive flying trials and development unit for both versions with RN, RM and Army Air Corps personnel. Both squadrons are based at RNAS Yeovilton and, under present plans, all future RN and Army Lynx units are to be based there. Unlike other Fleet Air Arm aircraft, 847 NAS aircraft will have ROYAL MARINES painted on their sides.

OTHER AIRCRAFT TYPES IN ROYAL NAVY SERVICE DURING 2014

CROWN COPYRIGHT/MoD 2011

Beech AVENGER T1

Engines 2 x Pratt & Whitney PT 6A turboprops.
Crew 1 or 2 pilots; up to 4 student observers plus instructors.
Squadron Service 750 Naval Air Squadron

Notes
Four aircraft are operated by 750 NAS as part of the Observer School at RNAS Culdrose for the third phase of training. The first two phases are flown in 703 NAS.

LEE HOWARD

GROB TUTOR T1

Engine 1 x Lycoming 0 - 360 - A1B6 piston engine
Crew 1 or 2 pilots
Squadron Service 703. 727 Naval Air Squadrons

Notes

703 NAS at RAF Barkston Heath carries out elementary training for RN and RM pilots. 727 NAS at RNAS Yeovilton carries out flying grading of newly entered aircrew and other light fixed-wing tasks.

Eurocopter SQUIRREL HT1

Engine 1 x Turbomeca Ariel 1D1
Crew 1 or 2 pilots and up to 4 passengers
Squadron Service 705 Naval Air Squadron

Notes

705 NAS provides basic helicopter training for RN and RM pilots as part of the Defence Helicopter Flying School at RAF Shawbury..

LEE HOWARD

Eurocopter AS365N DAUPHIN 2

Engines 2 x Turbomeca Arriel 1C1.
Crew 1 or 2 pilots.
Squadron Service Civil-owned, military registered

Notes
Two of these helicopters are based at Newquay Airport and flown in support of FOST activities in the Plymouth areas.

Royal Navy Historic Flight

Notes

Based at RNAS Yeovilton, the Flight includes Swordfish I W 5856; Swordfish II LS 326; Sea Fury FB 11 VR 930; Sea Fury T 20 VX 281; Sea Hawk WV 908 and Chipmunk T 10 WK 608. They are flown in displays by naval pilots and maintained by civilians under a MoD contract but are seldom all serviceable at the same time.

UNMANNED AIR VEHICLES

The RN procured an undisclosed number of ScanEagle unmanned air vehicle systems in 2013 under a 'contractor-owned and operated' deal with Boeing but a shortage of manpower has prevented the training of naval safety officers capable of 'flying' the aircraft from ships. This has delayed the first deployment but it is hoped to get the system to sea in 2014. First evaluated from HMS SUTHERLAND in 2006, a ScanEagle air vehicle can stay airborne for 15 to 18 hours up to 70 miles from its launcher unit, transmitting information from a video or infra-red camera. It weighs 48lb with a wingspan of 10 feet, is launched from a portable pneumatic catapult and recovered by catching a vertical wire attached to the launcher unit with hooks on the wingtips. It is 'flown' throughout its mission by a pilot in the parent ship.

The RN has shown interest in procuring an unmanned helicopter capable of embarked operation and hopes to evaluate potential designs during 2014.

A variety of unmanned aerial targets, including the Galileo Mirach 100/5, are provided for the British armed forces world-wide by the Combined Aerial Target Service, CATS, operated by QinetiQ.

ARMY AIR CORPS AND ROYAL AIR FORCE HELICOPTERS THAT CAN BE EMBARKED AS PART OF A TAILORED AIR GROUP

STEVE WRIGHT

AGUSTAWESTLAND APACHE AH 1

Notes Army Air Corps Apaches can be armed with up to 16 AGM-114 Hellfire missiles or up to 76 CRV-7 unguided rocket projectiles plus a single M230 30mm cannon with 1,160 rounds. Operated as part of the Joint Helicopter Force.

LEE HOWARD

BOEING CHINOOK

Notes RAF Chinooks are able to carry up to 44 fully equipped troops or a 20,000lb load and are armed with miniguns to give suppressive fire in assault landings. Operated as part of the Joint Helicopter Force.

WEAPONS OF THE ROYAL NAVY

Sea Launched Missiles

Trident II D5

The American built Lockheed Martin Trident 2 (D5) submarine launched strategic missiles are Britain's only nuclear weapons and form the UK contribution to the NATO strategic deterrent. 16 missiles, each capable of carrying up to 6 UK manufactured thermonuclear warheads (but currently limited to 4 under current government policy), can be carried aboard each of the Vanguard class SSBNs. Trident has a maximum range of 12,000 km and is powered by a three stage rocket motor. Launch weight is 60 tonnes, overall length and width are 13.4 metres and 2.1 metres respectively.

Tomahawk (BGM-109)

This is a land attack cruise missile with a range of 1600 km and can be launched from a variety of platforms including surface ships and submarines. Some 65 of the latter version were purchased from America to arm Trafalgar class SSNs with the first being delivered to the Royal Navy for trials during 1998. Tomahawk is fired in a disposal container from the submarine's conventional torpedo tubes and is then accelerated to its subsonic cruising speed by a booster rocket motor before a lightweight F-107 turbojet takes over for the cruise. Its extremely accurate guidance system means that small targets can be hit with precision at maximum range, as was dramatically illustrated in the Gulf War and Afghanistan. Total weight of the submarine version, including its launch capsule is 1816 kg, it carries a 450 kg warhead, length is 6.4 metres and wingspan (fully extended) 2.54 m. Fitted in Astute & T class submarines.

Harpoon

The Harpoon is a sophisticated anti-ship missile using a combination of inertial guidance and active radar homing to attack targets out to a range of 130 km, cruising at Mach 0.9 and carrying a 227 kg warhead. It is powered by a lightweight turbojet but is accelerated at launch by a booster rocket. Fitted to Type 23 frigates, it is also the intention to refit four of the Type 45 destroyers with the systems removed from the decommissioned Batch III Type 22 frigates.

Sea Viper (Aster 15/30)

Two versions of the Aster missile will equip the Type 45 Destroyer, the shorter range Aster 15 and the longer range Aster 30. The missiles form the weapon component of the Principal Anti Air Missile System (PAAMS). Housed in a 48 cell Sylver Vertical Launch system, the missile mix can be loaded to match the ships requirement. Aster 15 has a range of 30 km while Aster 30 can achieve 100 km. The prime external difference between the two is the size of the booster rocket attached to the bottom of the missile. PAAMS is known as Sea Viper in RN service.

Sea Wolf

Short range rapid reaction anti-missile missile and anti-aircraft weapon. The complete weapon system, including radars and fire control computers, is entirely automatic in operation. Type 23 frigates carry 32 Vertical Launch Seawolf (VLS) in a silo on the foredeck. Basic missile data: weight 82 kg, length 1.9 m, wingspan 56 cm, range c.5-6 km, warhead 13.4 kg. The VLS missile is basically similar but has jettisonable tandem boost rocket motors.

Air Launched Missiles

Sea Skua

A small anti-ship missile developed by British Aerospace arming the Lynx helicopters carried by various frigates and destroyers. The missile weighs 147 kg, has a length of 2.85 m and a span of 62 cm. Powered by solid fuel booster and sustainer rocket motors, it has a range of over 15 km at high subsonic speed. Sea Skua is particularly effective against patrol vessels and fast attack craft, as was demonstrated in both the Falklands and Gulf Wars.

Guns

114mm Vickers Mk8 Mod 1

The Royal Navy's standard medium calibre general purpose gun which arms the Type 23 frigates and Type 45 destroyers. The Mod 1 is an electrically operated version of the original gun and is recognised by its angular turret. First introduced in 2001 it is now fitted in all Type 23 and Type 45 vessels. Rate of fire: 25 rounds/min. Range: 22,000 m. Weight of Shell: 21 kg.

Goalkeeper

A highly effective automatic Close in Weapons System (CIWS) designed to shoot down missiles and aircraft which have evaded the outer layers of a ships defences. The complete system, designed and built in Holland, is on an autonomous mounting and includes radars, fire control computers and a 7-barrel 30 mm Gatling gun firing 4200 rounds/min. Goalkeeper is designed to engage targets between 350 and 1500 metres away.

Phalanx

A US built CIWS designed around the Vulcan 20 mm rotary cannon. Rate of fire is 3000 rounds/min and effective range is c.1500 m. Fitted in Type 45, OCEAN and some Wave, Bay and Fort classes. Block 1B began entering service from 2009. Incorporates side mounted Forward looking infra-red enabling CIWS to engage low aircraft and surface craft. In October 2012 it was announced that a further five Phalanx Block 1B mountings were to be procured to protect RFA ships

DS30B 30mm

Single mounting carrying an Oerlikon 30mm gun. Fitted to Type 23 frigates and various patrol vessels and MCMVs. In August 2005 it was announced that the DS30B fitted in Type 23 frigates was to be upgraded to DS30M Mk 2 to include new direct-drive digital servos and the replacement of the earlier Oerlikon KCB cannon with the ATK Mk 44 Bushmaster II 30 mm gun. Consideration is already being given to purchasing additional DS30M Mk 2 systems for minor war vessels and auxiliaries.

GAM BO 20mm

A simple hand operated mounting carrying a single Oerlikon KAA 200 automatic cannon firing 1000 rounds/min. Maximum range is 2000 m. Carried by most of the fleet's major warships except the Type 23 frigates.

20mm Mk.7A

The design of this simple but reliable weapon dates back to World War II but it still provides a useful increase in firepower, particularly for auxiliary vessels and RFAs. Rate of fire 500-800 rounds/min.

Close Range Weapons

In addition to the major weapons systems, all RN ships carry a variety of smaller calibre weapons to provide protection against emerging terrorist threats in port and on the high seas such as small fast suicide craft. In addition it is sometimes preferable, during policing or stop and search operations to have a smaller calibre weapon available. Depending upon the operational environment ships may be seen armed with varying numbers of pedestal mounted General Purpose Machine Guns (GPMG). Another addition to the close in weapons is the Mk 44 Mini Gun a total of 150 of which have been procured from the United States as a fleetwide fit. Fitted to a naval post mount, the Minigun is able to fire up to 3,000 rounds per minute, and is fully self-contained (operating off battery power).

Torpedoes

Stingray

A lightweight anti-submarine torpedo which can be launched from ships, helicopters or aircraft. In effect it is an undersea guided missile with a range of 11 km at 45 knots or 7.5 km at 60 knots. Length 2.1 m, diameter 330 mm. Type 23s have the Magazine Torpedo Launch System (MTLS) with internal launch tubes. Sting Ray Mod 1 is intended to prosecute the same threats as the original Sting Ray but with an enhanced capability against small conventionally powered submarines and an improved shallow-water performance.

Spearfish

Spearfish is a submarine-launched heavyweight torpedo which has replaced Tigerfish. Claimed by the manufacturers to be the world's fastest torpedo, capable of over 70 kts, its sophisticated guidance system includes an onboard acoustic processing suite and tactical computer backed up by a command and control wire link to the parent submarine. Over 20ft in length and weighing nearly two tons, Spearfish is fired from the standard 21-inch submarine torpedo tube and utilises an advanced bi-propellant gas turbine engine for higher performance.

Future Weapons

Future Anti-Surface Guided Weapon (Heavy)

This project, led by MBDA (UK) and derived from the company's existing 15km range Sea Skua Anti-Ship Missile, will provide the lead in to a 100kg weapon family that will include the Selected Precision Effects at Range (SPEAR) air-launched weapon for the Royal Air Force.

Using an Imaging Infra Red (IIR) seeker capability, the project will be developed in collaboration with France, which has a similar anti-ship missile requirement, the Anti Navire Léger. It will provide the main armament for the RN's AW159 Lynx Wildcat and the French Navy's NH90 and Panther helicopters.

Future Anti-Surface Guided Weapon (Light)

Led by Thales (UK), this project will be based on the company's 6-8km range Lightweight Multi-role Missile (LMM) and will replace the Sea Skua. The new 30kg class warhead is designed to defeat Fast Attack Craft ranging from 50 to 500 tonnes, corvettes, static coastal and land targets and severely damage and immobilise larger craft via precision aim point selection. With a long stand-off capability, the launch helicopter will be able to remain safely outside of enemy air defences. The RN variant is being developed to operate from the AW159 Lynx Wildcat helicopter.

Sea Ceptor (formerly known as FLAADS-M)

Incorporating the Common Anti-Air Modular Missile (CAAMM) family, being developed to replace the Rapier and Seawolf SAM systems, plus the ASRAAM short range Air-to-Air Missile. It will arm the Royal Navy's Type 23 frigates and its Type 26 Global Combat Ships. In Spring 2012 the MoD awarded MBDA UK a five-year Demonstration Phase contract worth £483 million to develop the missile for the RN. In September 2013 a £250 million contract was announced to manufacture the missile in the UK, sustaining around 250 jobs at MBDA sites in Stevenage, Filton and Lostock. Installation of the Sea Ceptor on Type 23 frigates is due to start in 2015 and be completed by 2021.

At the end of the line ...

Readers may well find other warships afloat which are not mentioned in this book. The majority have fulfilled a long and useful life and are now relegated to non-seagoing duties. The following list gives details of their current duties:

Pennant No	Ship	Remarks
	BRITANNIA	Ex Royal Yacht at Leith. Open to the public.
	CAROLINE	Light Cruiser and veteran of the Battle of Jutland. Is to be restored and opened in 2014 as a tourist attraction at Belfast.
M29	BRECON	Hunt Class Minehunter - Attached to the New Entry Training Establishment, HMS RALEIGH, Torpoint, as a static Seamanship Training ship.
M103	CROMER	Single Role Minehunter - Attached to Britannia Royal Naval College, Dartmouth as a Static Training Ship.
L3505	SIR TRISTRAM	Refitted as a Static Range Vessel at Portland.
C35	BELFAST	World War II Cruiser Museum ship - Pool of London. Open to the public daily. Tel: 020 7940 6300
D23	BRISTOL	Type 82 Destroyer - Sea Cadet Training Ship at Portsmouth.
D73 S17	CAVALIER OCELOT	World War II Destroyer & Oberon class Submarine Museum Ships at Chatham. Open to the public. Tel: 01634 823800
F126 M1115	PLYMOUTH BRONINGTON	The ships remain at Birkenhead whilst discussions over their future continue.
S67	ALLIANCE	Submarine - Museum Ship at Gosport Open to the public daily. Tel: 023 92 511349
S50	COURAGEOUS	Nuclear-powered Submarine - On display at Devonport Naval Base. Can be visited during Base Tours. Tel: 01752 552326 for details.
M1151	IVESTON	Static Sea Cadet Training Vessel (Thurrock)
S21	ONYX	At Barrow awaiting a new future as a proposed Submarine Heritage Centre will not now be opened.

At the time of publishing (December 2013) the following ships were laid up in long term storage or awaiting sale.

PORTSMOUTH: Gloucester; Manchester; York; Edinburgh; Liverpool; Walney.

PLYMOUTH: Trafalgar; Turbulent; Sceptre; Superb; Splendid; Spartan; Sovereign; Conqueror; Valiant; Warspite.

ROSYTH: Resolution; Renown; Repulse; Revenge; Swiftsure; Churchill; Dreadnought.

Since the previous edition the following vessels in long term storage or awaiting scrap were disposed of:

FORT GEORGE: Departed Liverpool under tow of tug CHRISTOS XXIII on 16 January 2013 bound for recycling at Leyal Shipbreakers, Turkey.

ARK ROYAL: Departed Portsmouth under tow of tug CHRISTOS XXIII on 20 May 2013 bound for recycling at Leyal Shipbreakers, Turkey.

CHATHAM: Departed Portsmouth under tow of tug HELLAS on 8 October 2013 bound for recycling at Leyal Shipbreakers, Turkey (see photo above).

CAMPBELTOWN: Departed Portsmouth under tow of tug CHRISTOS XXIV on 15 October 2013 bound for recycling at Leyal Shipbreakers, Turkey.

CORNWALL: Departed Portsmouth under tow of tug NEPTUN 10 on 24 October 2013 bound for recycling at Swansea, Wales.

CUMBERLAND: Departed Portsmouth under tow of tug SPARTAN on 4 November 2013 bound for recycling at Leyal Shipbreakers, Turkey.